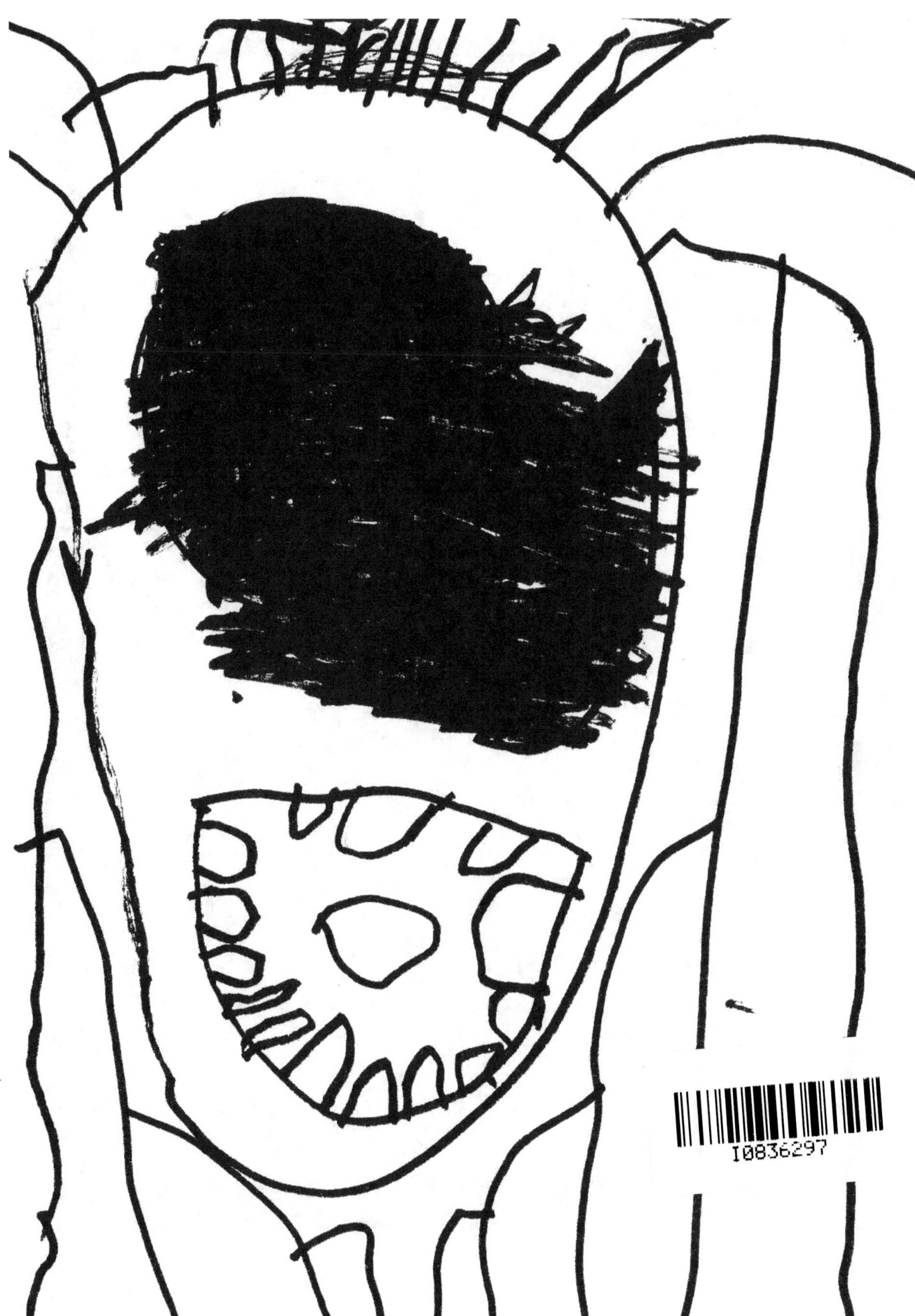

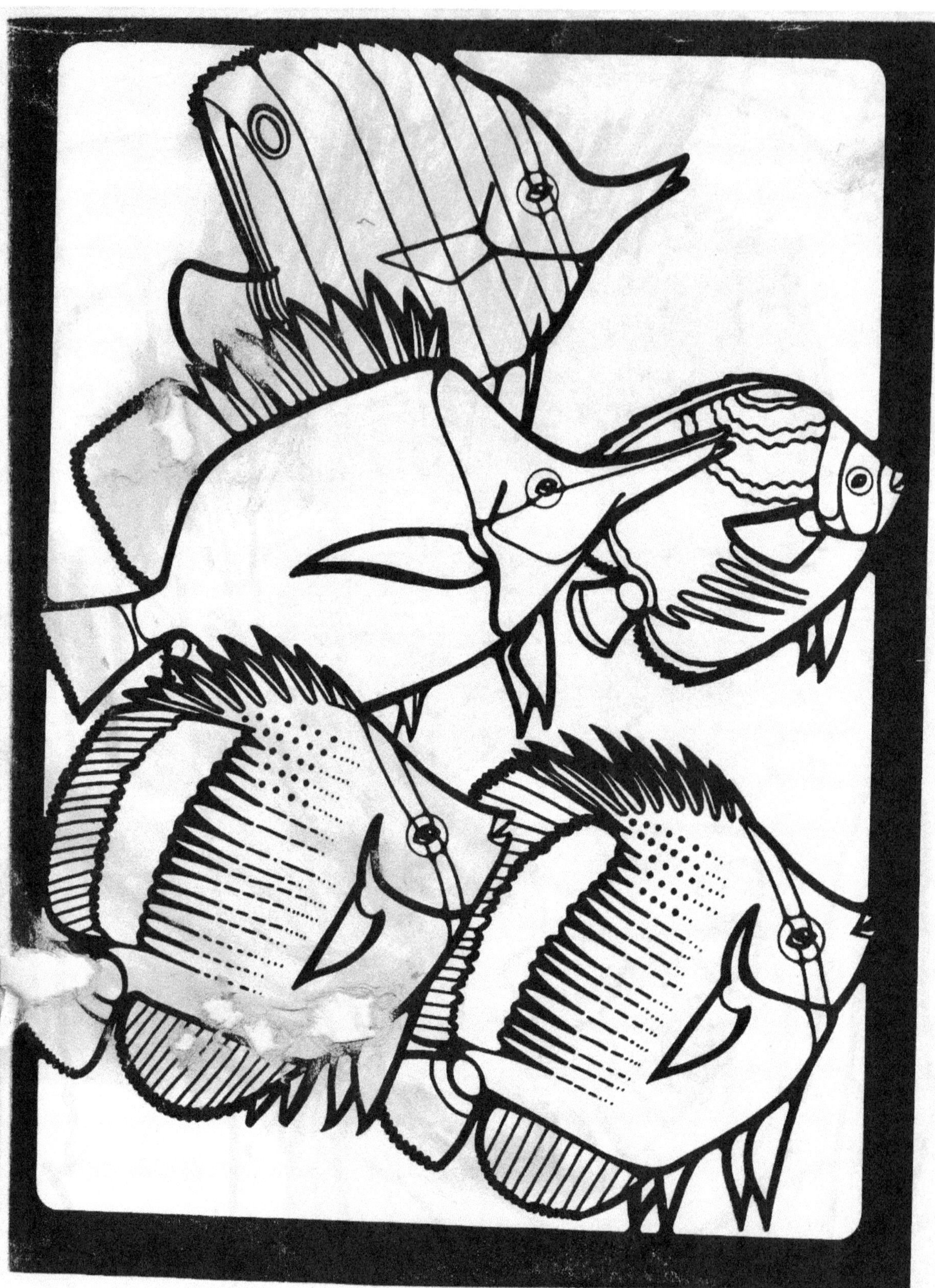

MT in 5

MT in 5 by MT (Matthew Thomas) Stolte

With collaborations by Andrew Topel, C. Mehrl Bennett & John M. Bennett

Endpapers by "the new mailart generation in town" via Mindaugas Žuromskas, Lithuania, sent February 24, 2022 marking "the Russian attack on Ukraine" – coloring book fish printouts from M.M.H.I. 1998

ISBN: 978-1-7353850-4-4

First Edition

eMTeVisPub

http://www.lulu.com/spotlight/emtevispub
https://www.freewebs.com/matthewstolte/

This book was made possible in part by generous grants from Dane Arts.

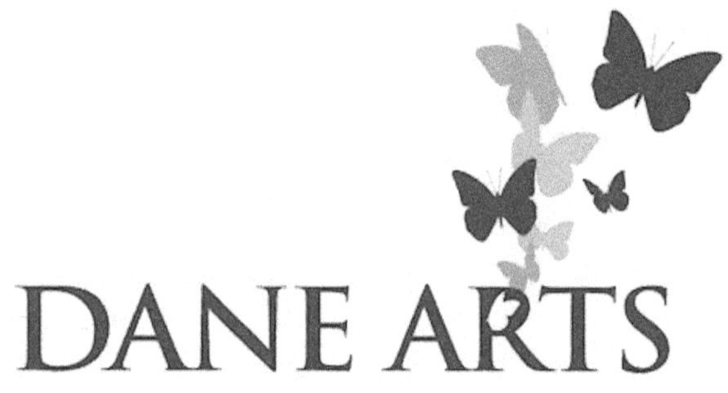

for Harper, Jace, Vaughn & Griffin

1

MadPo

One of the most frustrating things that ever happened to me was when I was separated from the insane visual poetry I made during my 1st episode of mania the summer of 1998. 24 years old, I was up for 7 days before being hospitalized. My poetic practice the beginning of that summer was writing haiku using magic markers. As the summer deepened & my mania grew, wildly scrawling haiku, I discovered writing was drawing – that my words were pictures – & by dotting letters you could make little men. But instead of simply making smiley faces, my words were alive fueled by mania. There *were* little men in my words – they moved & goofed around. The poetry I was making was not sane – combining symbols & letters – some works not unlike math poetry. A phrase I think of to describe these works is from a song by Arto Lindsay titled "Child Prodigy": "His own private math."

I made 100s of these poems in my mania – even wrote some on the wall. I was drawing poems on loose leaf paper & dropping them into a grocery bag. When I was in the hospital, I requested this bag of poems but was told it had been thrown away. This was the only thing of importance to me. In the hospital, I finally got some sleep, received medication & realized that I had gone crazy (I came out of my psychosis when a generation older than me artist named Jim showed me his marker made artworks taped up & down a wing of the floor). I lost the connection to the poems I had been making & without them, that connection was forever lost. Perhaps it was all nonsense. Perhaps not. I'll never know.

The initial artwork I made in the hospital was directly referencing insanity – a sort of symbolism for the insane that only made sense within the walls of the institution – like painting a single cloud up on a sheet of blank blue paper, for example. Or scribbling $s in green on sheets of paper & tossing them all over the floor. Something about golf. All I knew was that the poems had to "be painted."

Most of my initial shape poetry was akin to stick figures. These were the 1st poems I made that made sense. "Private math" gave way to shape poetry & concrete. I drew "Ego" in the hospital using a blue pencil. I consider it my 1st concrete poem. These works span just over a year's worth of time.

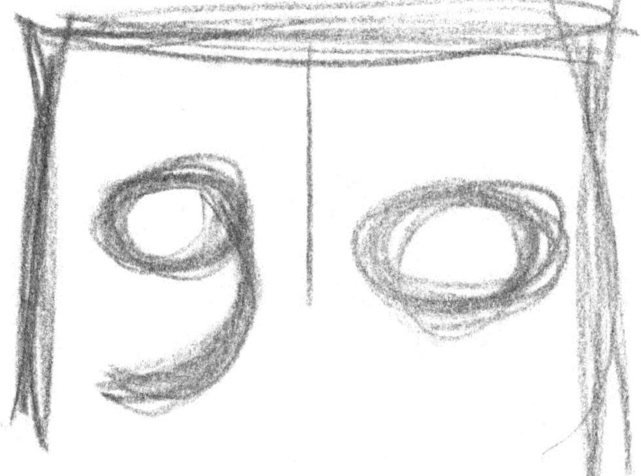

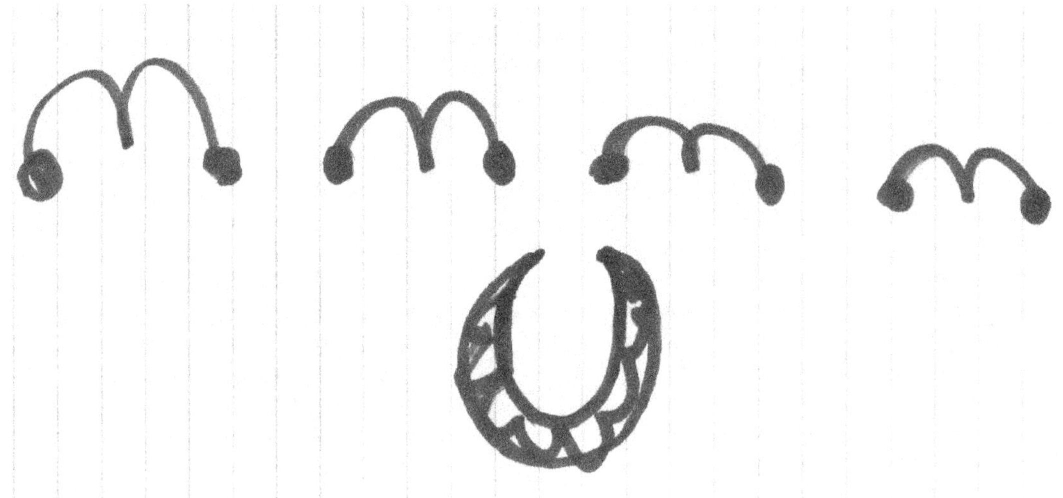

Pol a

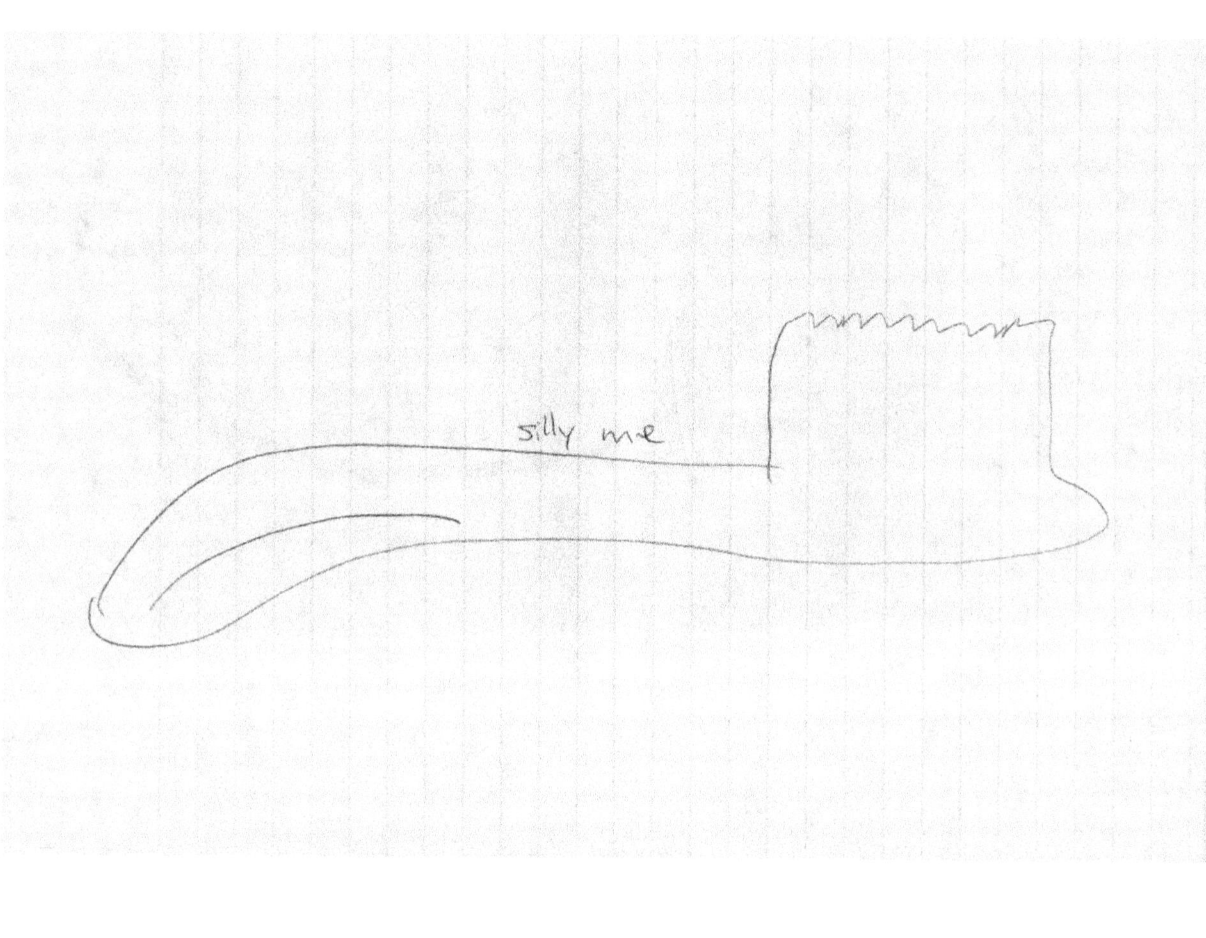
silly me

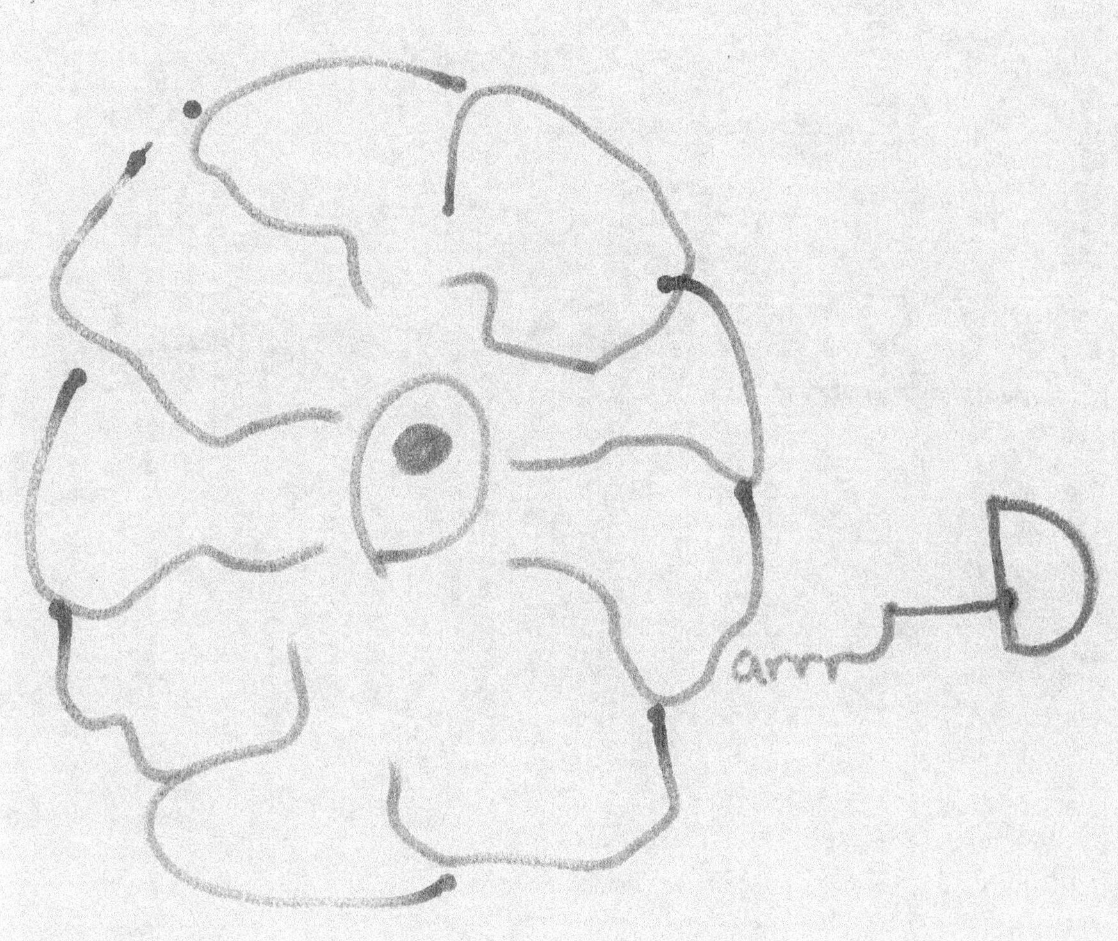
arrr

MUST arrrrr

fix

t

~~censored~~

drink

drink

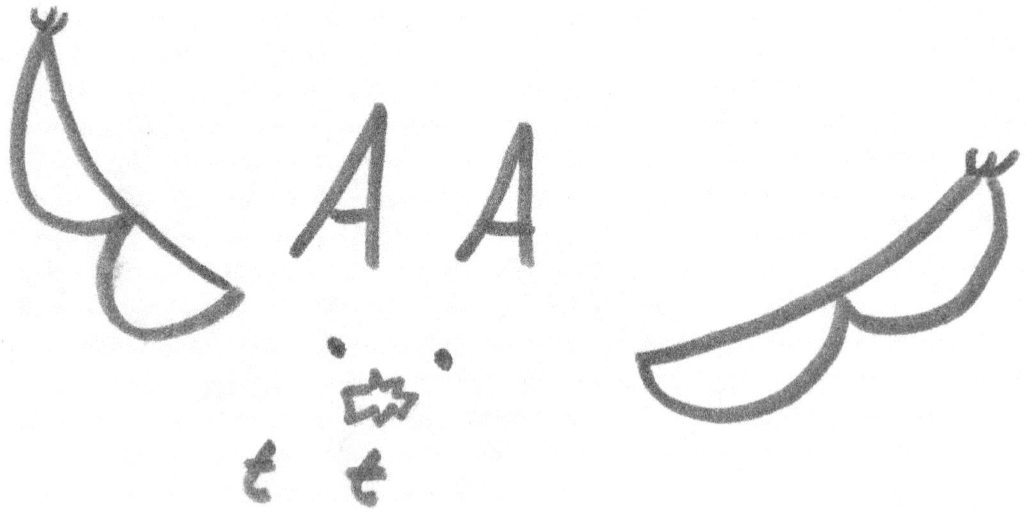

PEACE

tyger!

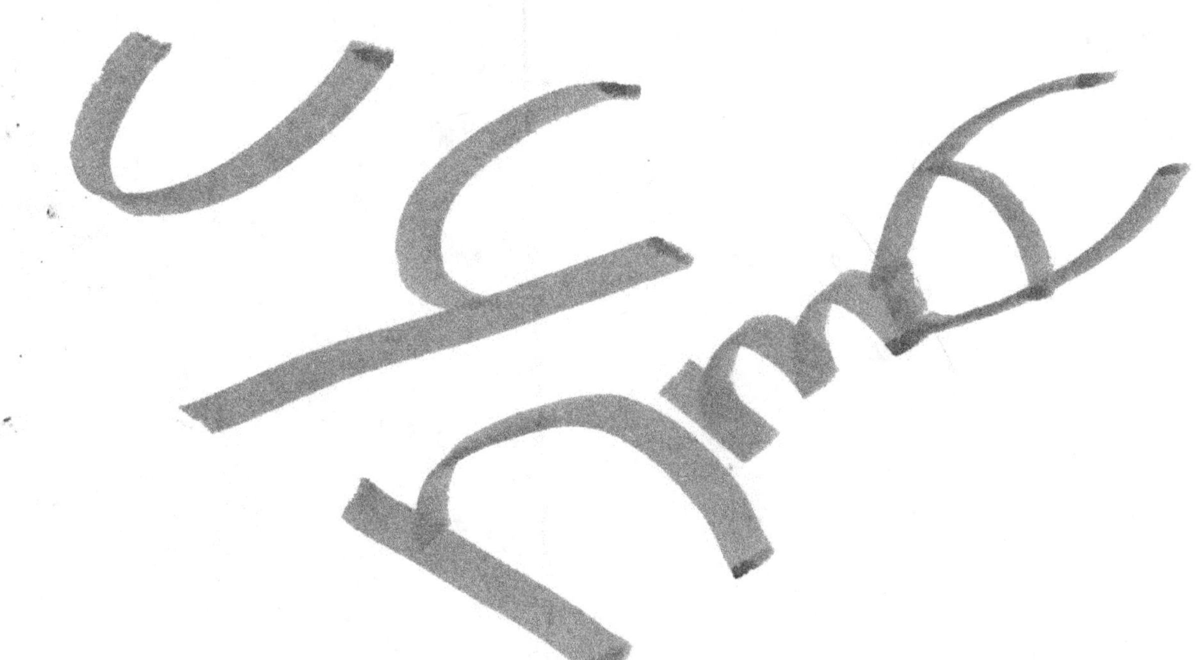

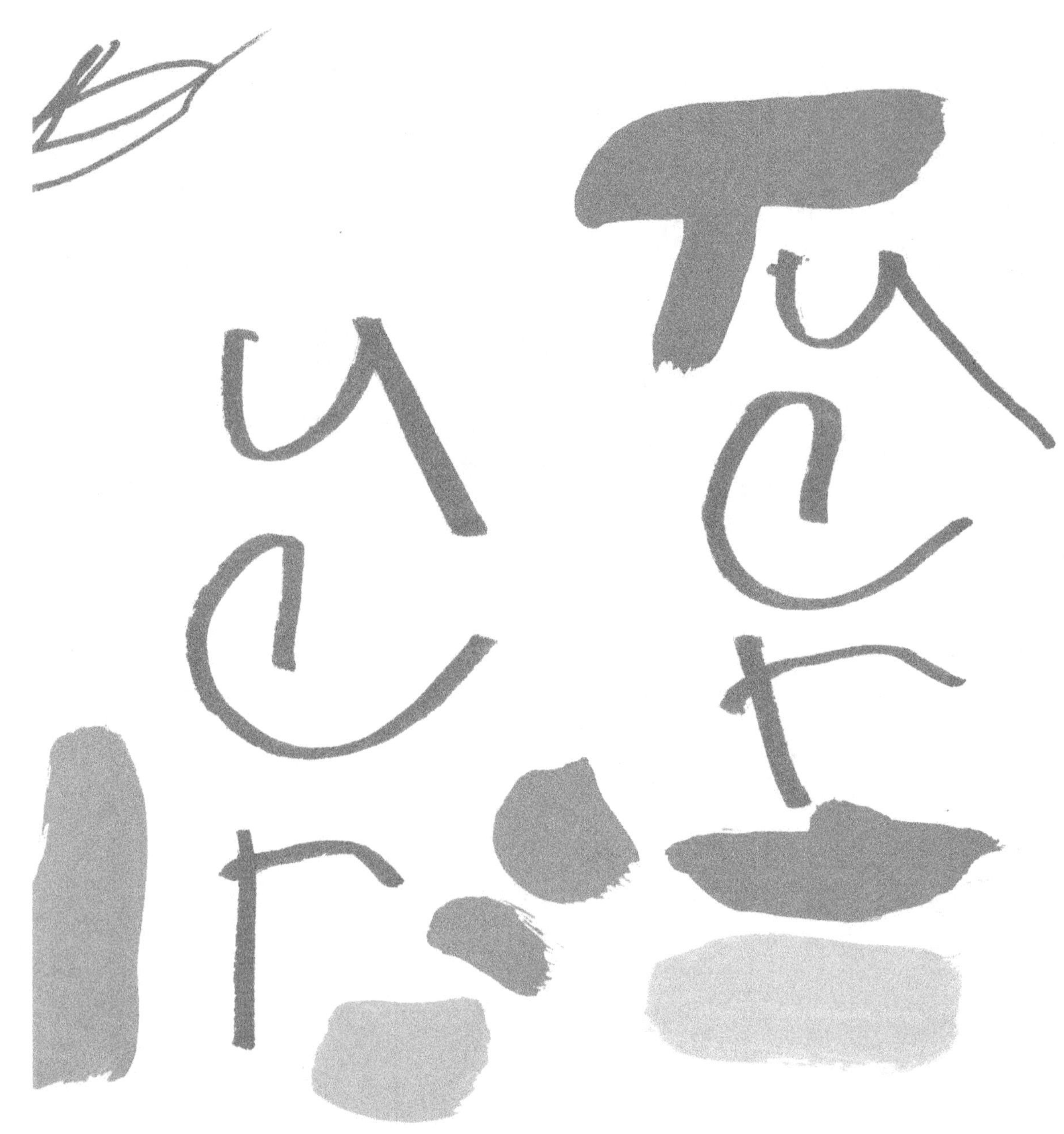

2

4 x 6 Stenciled $s & ¢s

December 2007, inspired by a small apartment, I used stencils on 4 x 6-inch index cards to paint my concrete $s & ¢s poems. I made perhaps a couple 100 of these. I framed them & gave them away. People enjoyed fingering through them & choosing their favorite. Some I sold. In 2009, mIEKAL aND published a couple in *Anthology Spidertangle*. In 2010 I published my 1st collection of this type of concrete poem (*Concrete Dollars and Cents Poems*) & made a failed attempt in 2011 to publish a collection of the stenciled version which follows.

I've found that only poets seem to appreciate the raw version of my $s & ¢s poems. What is easy for them seems opaque to the rest of the world.

4 x 6 POEMS

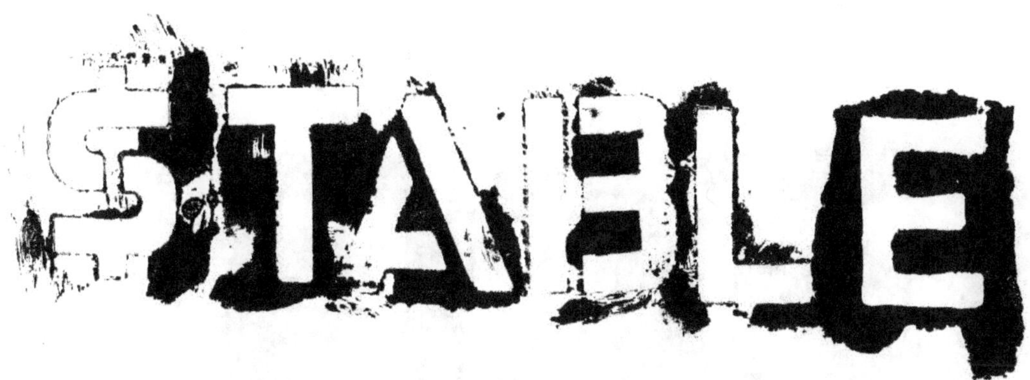
STABLE

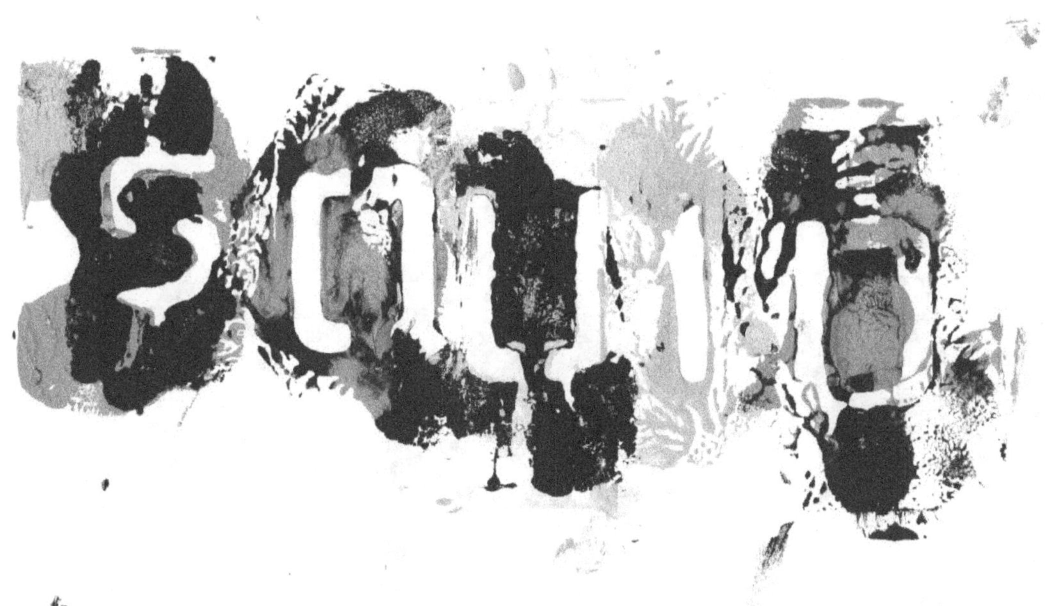

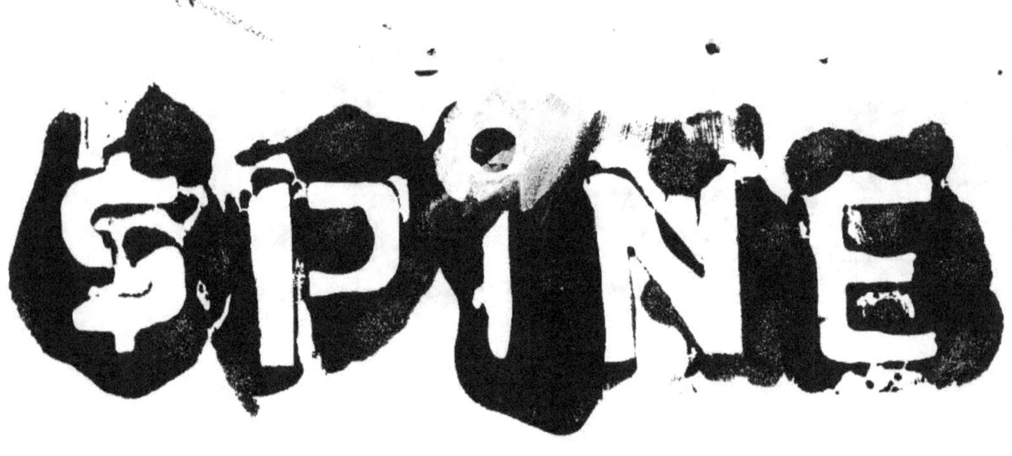
$PINE

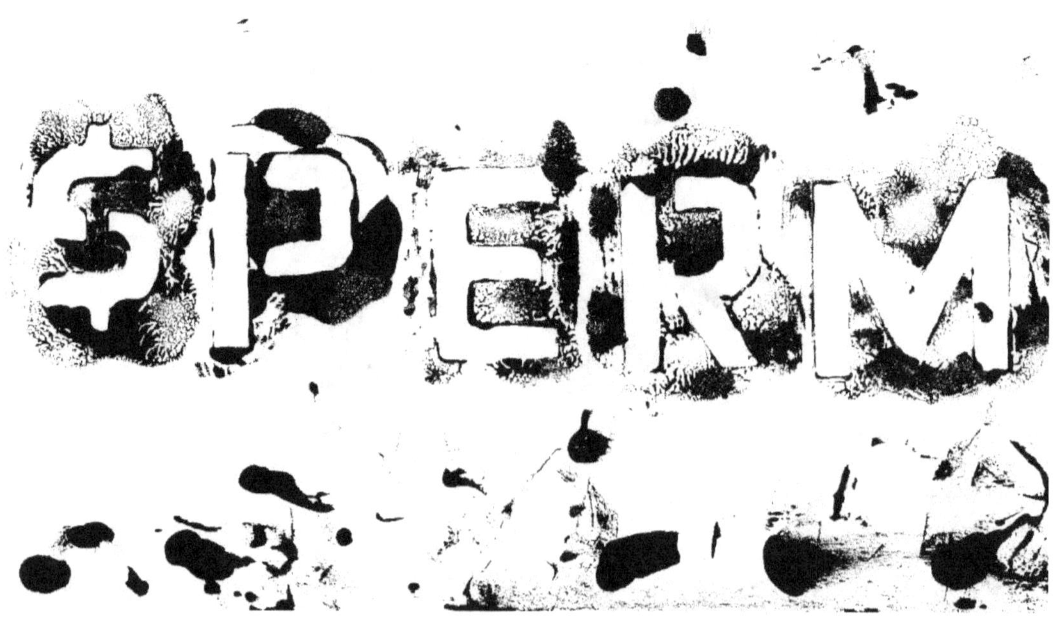
$PERM

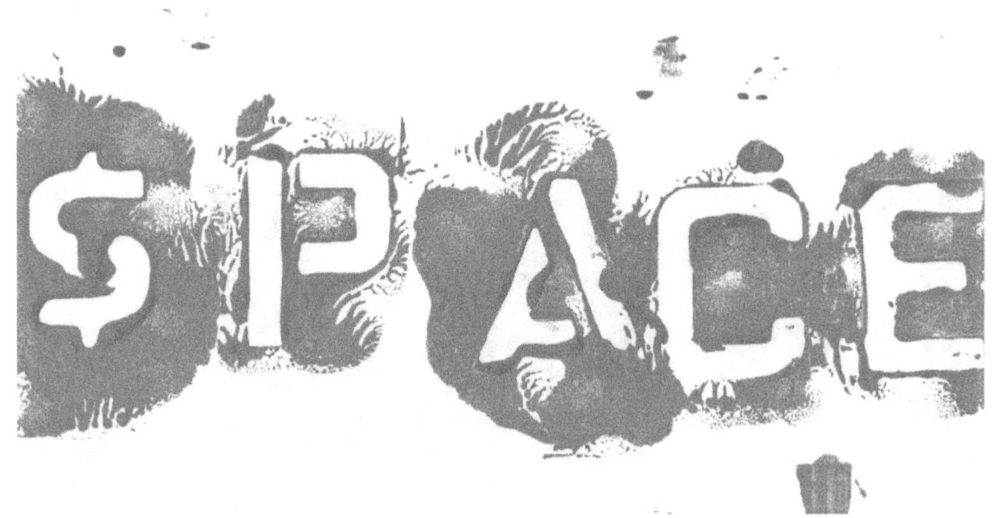
$PACE

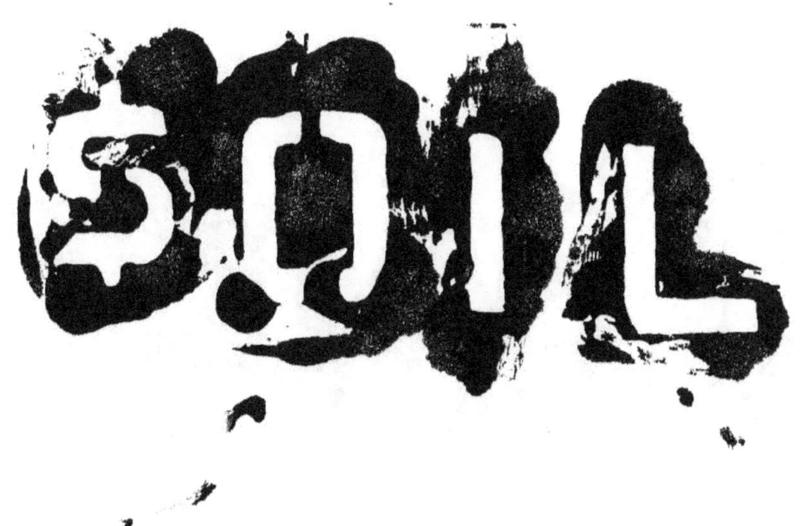
$OIL

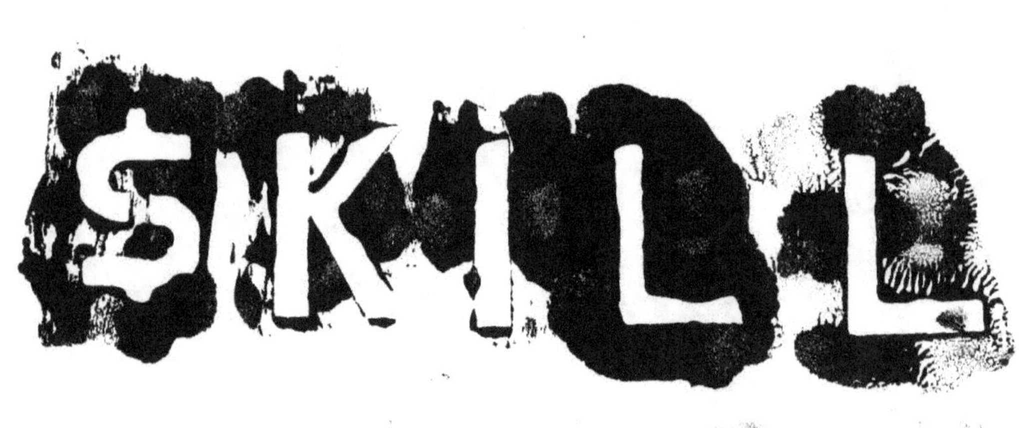
SKILL

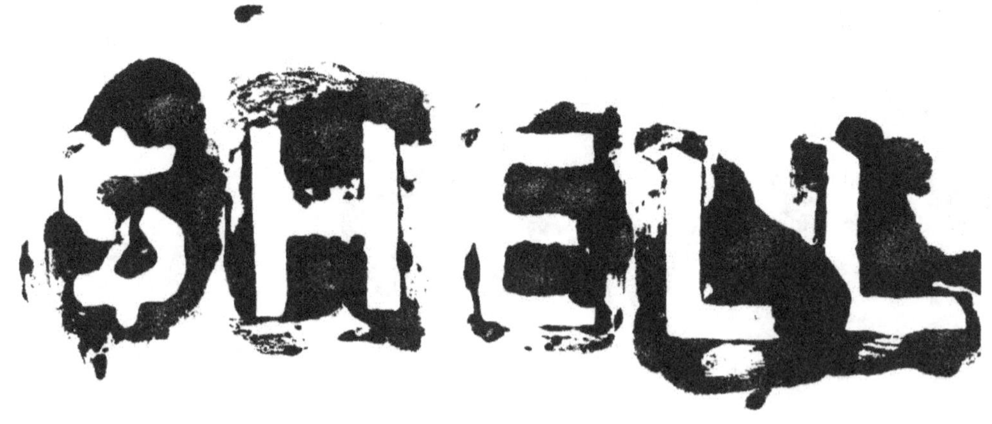
SHELL

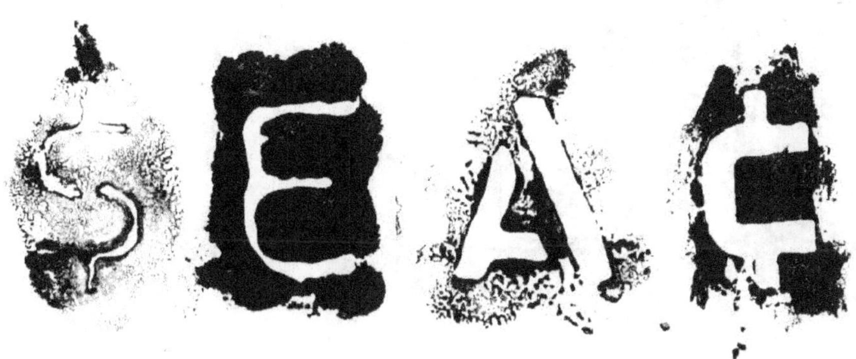
$EA¢

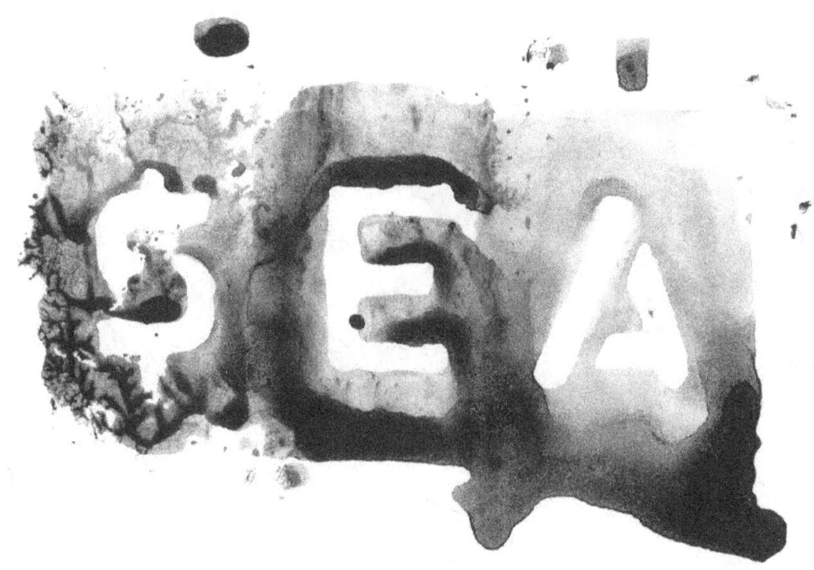
$EA

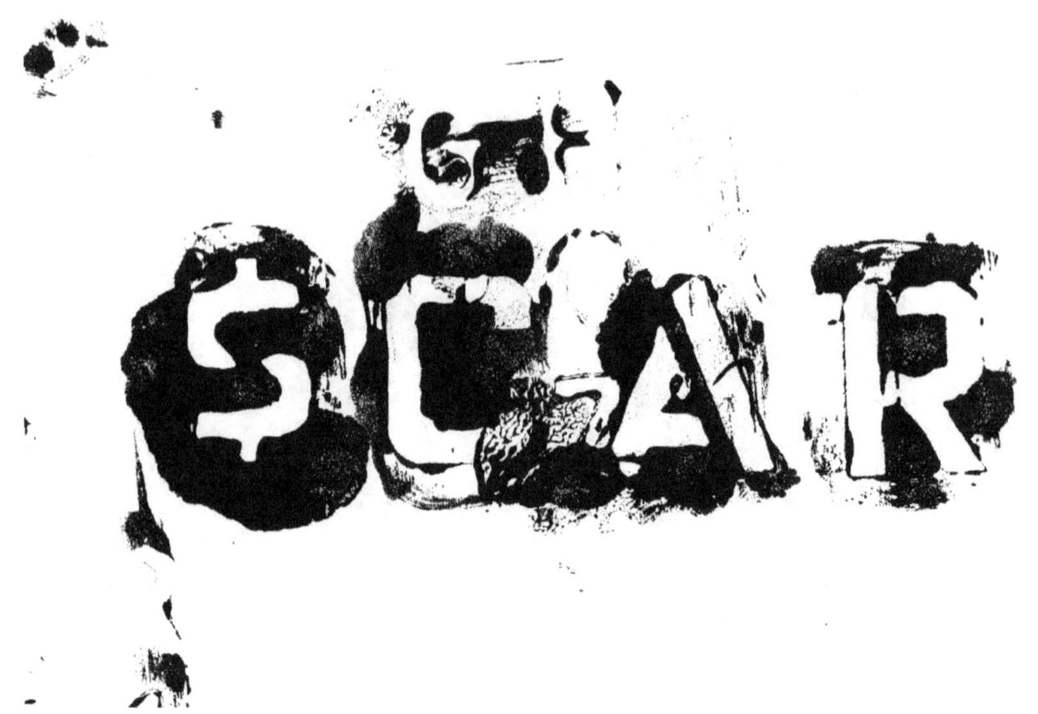
$CAR

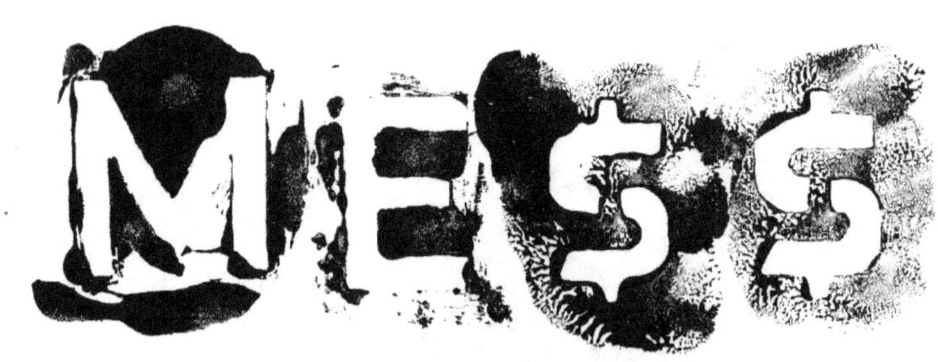
ME$$

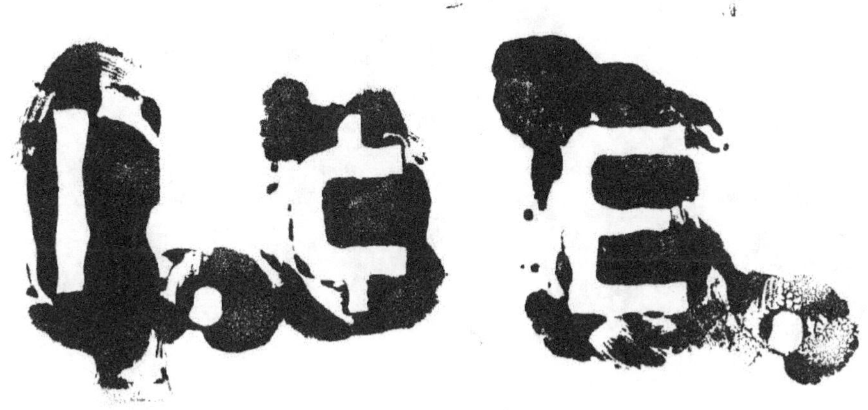

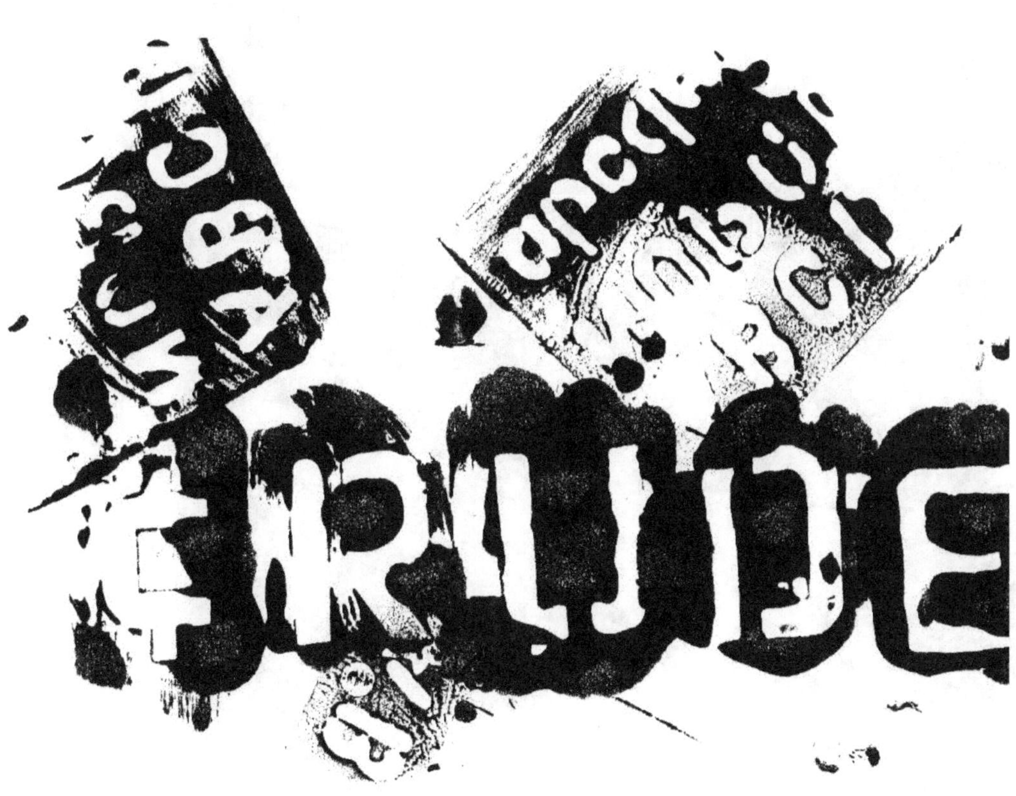

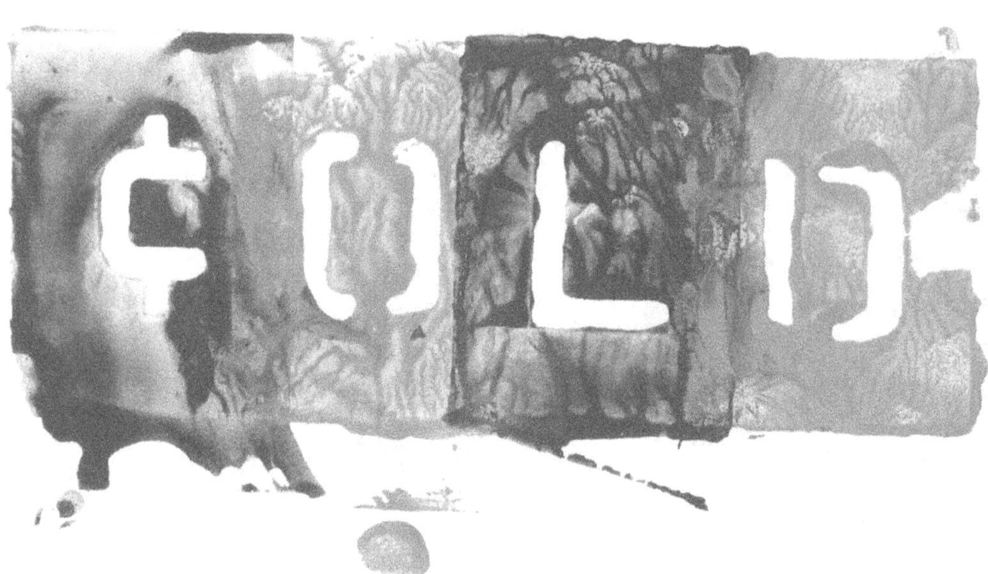
COLD

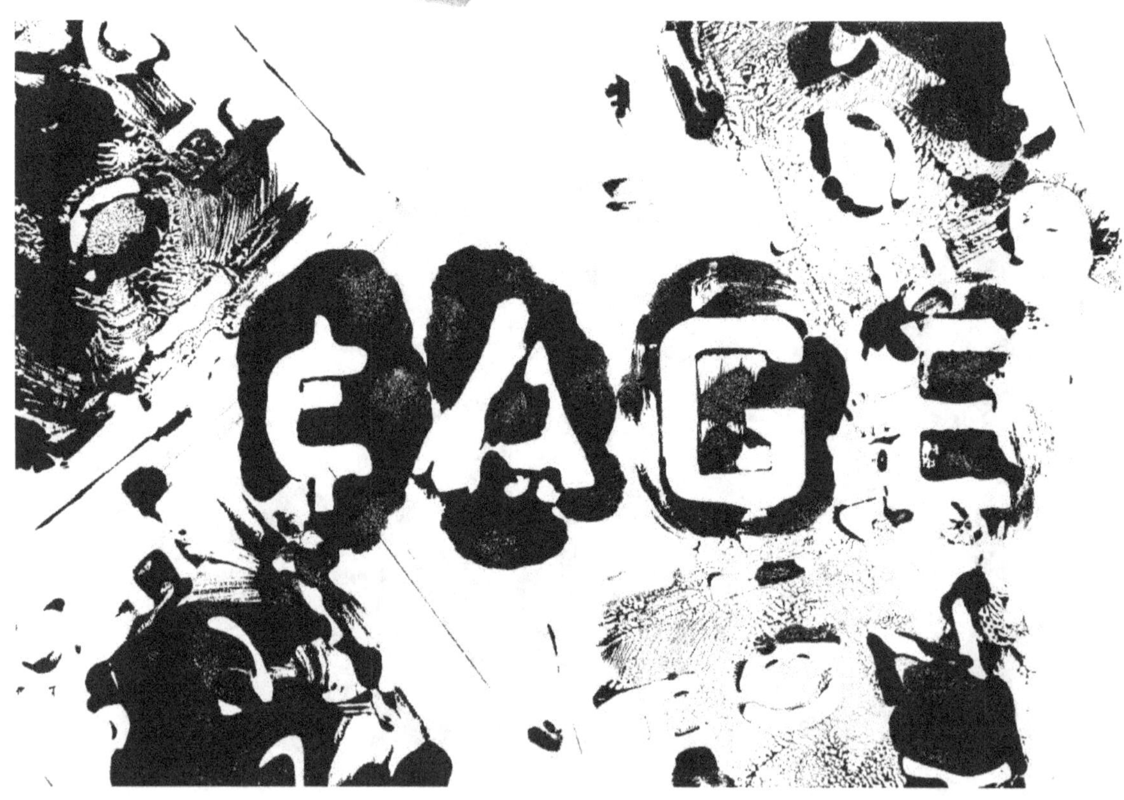
CAGE

3

D (or Moon) Poems

A large number of these D poems (or moon poems, made circa 2006) were rejected by a publisher of minimalist poetry because there wasn't enough there there. Like haiku & my $s & ¢s poems, there are 3 lines/ ideas to consider: the ½ moon, as represented by the letter D, & the full & broken word.

Why not give the moon back to language?

D

inner

D

i.e.

D

river

D

rain

D

rug

D

rape

D

raw

D

ate

D

a.m. age

D

owner

4

For Oceans (Oil Spill Works)

I sold my car in 2004 for environmental reasons (as well as an opportunity to learn how to ride the bus). I live in a city large enough to use public transportation. I believe my health, day to day experience & the environment are all better for it.

Before the *Deepwater Horizon* oil spill of 2010, I naively thought I could track oil spills around the world in order to wrap my head around the problem. I discovered that oil spills are not only frequent, but runoff happens every day & every so often we get a media attention grabbing record breaker oil spill, as in 2010. During the Gulf War in 1991, crude oil was purposely dumped into the Persian Gulf, one of the largest amounts of all time, considered an act of environmental terrorism.

Perhaps I was drawn to oil spills for their blunt aesthetic & result. But what are oil spills compared to climate change? The fashion industry & food waste?

These works were made circa 2010-2017.

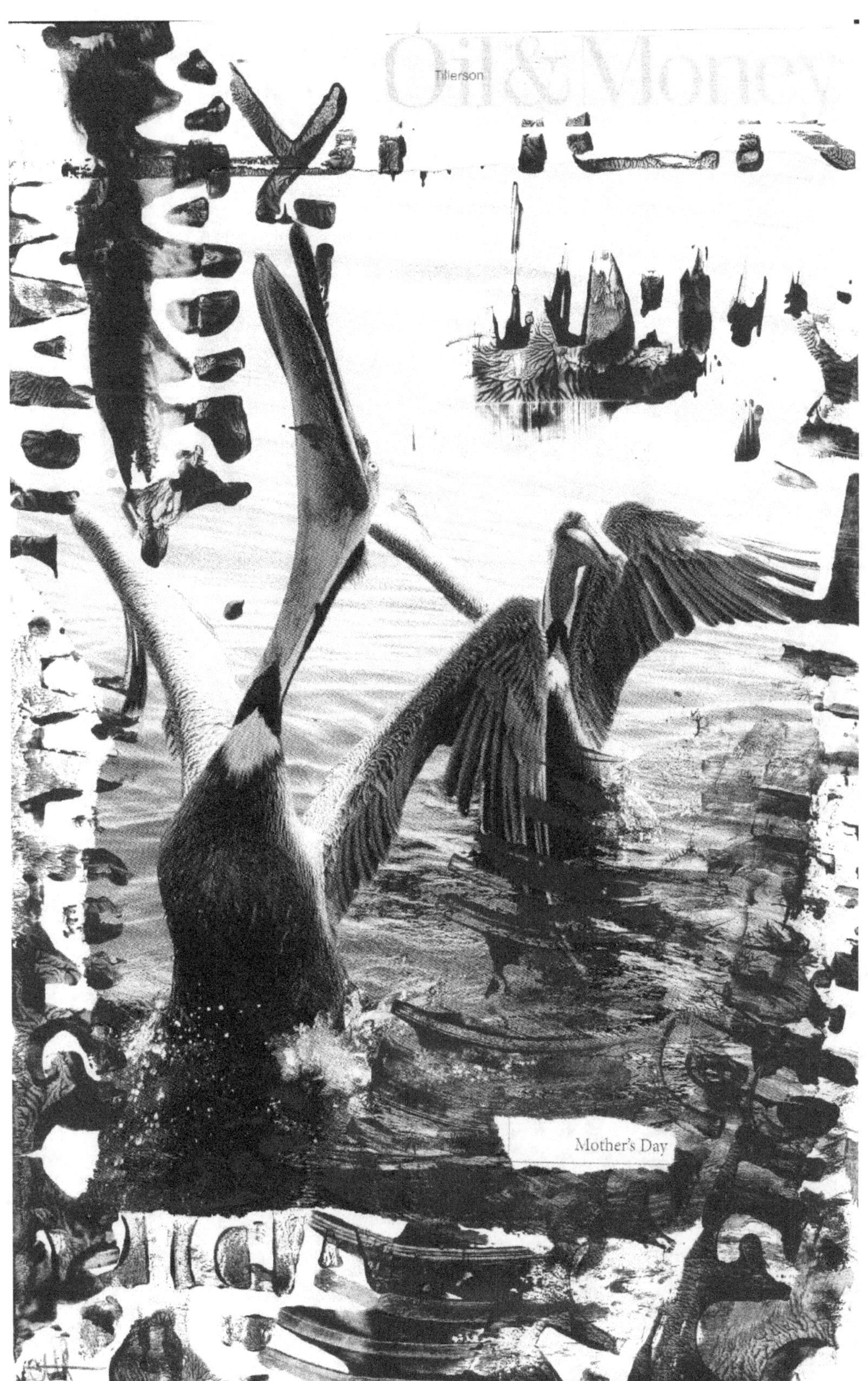
Oil & Money
Tillerson
Mother's Day

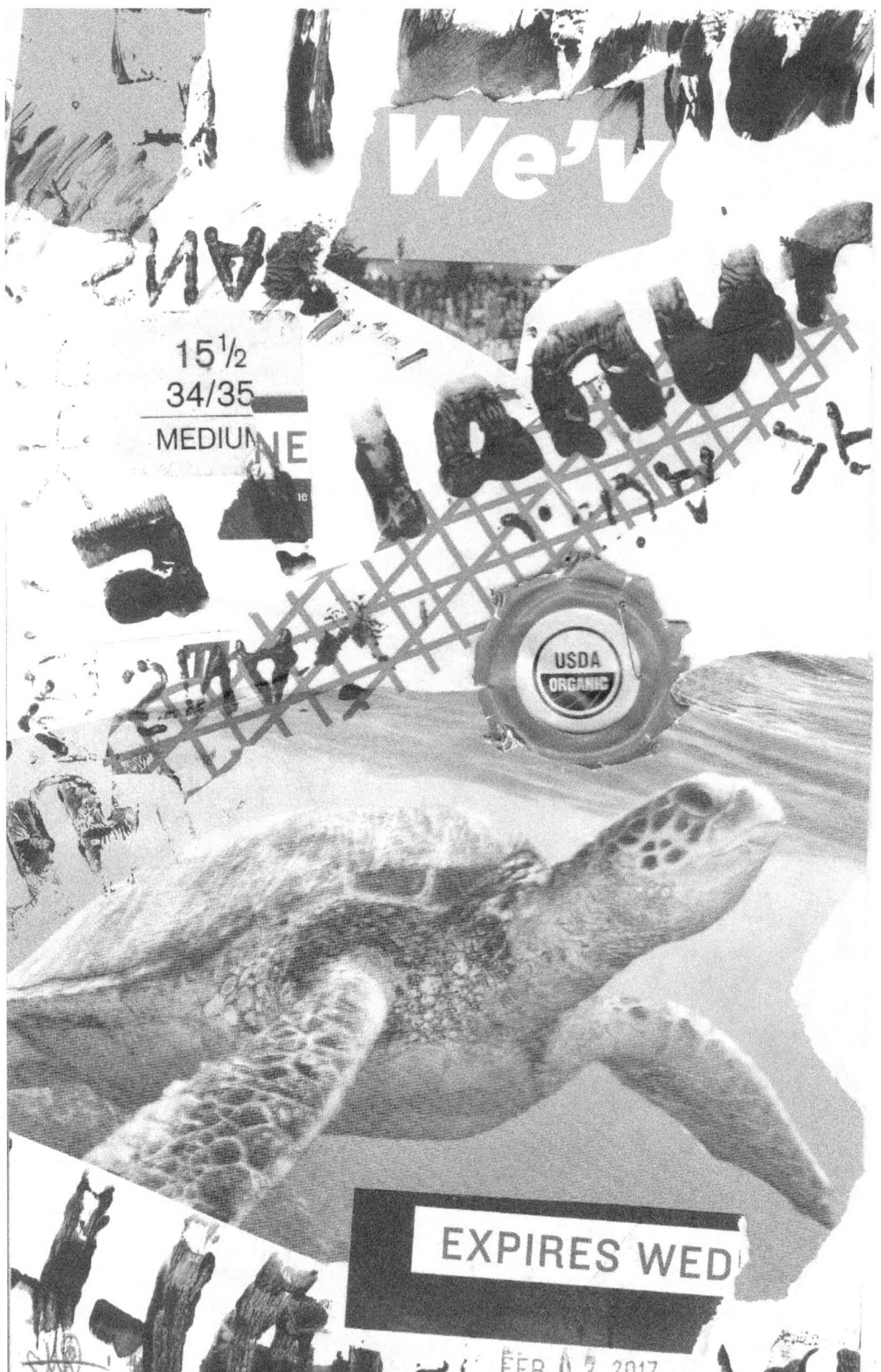
We'v
15½
34/35
MEDIUM
NE
USDA
ORGANIC
EXPIRES WED
FEB 07 2017

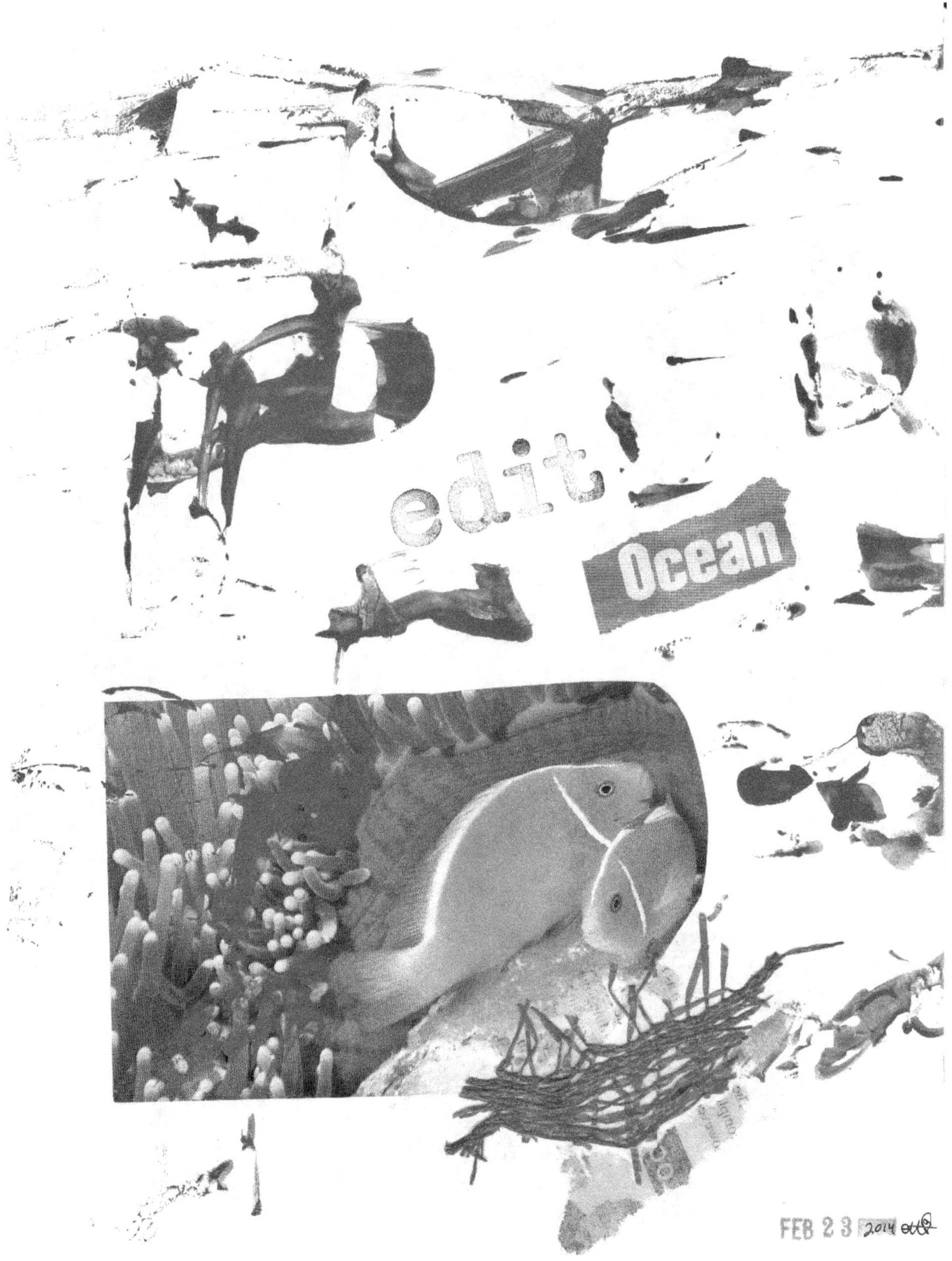

FEB 2 3 2014

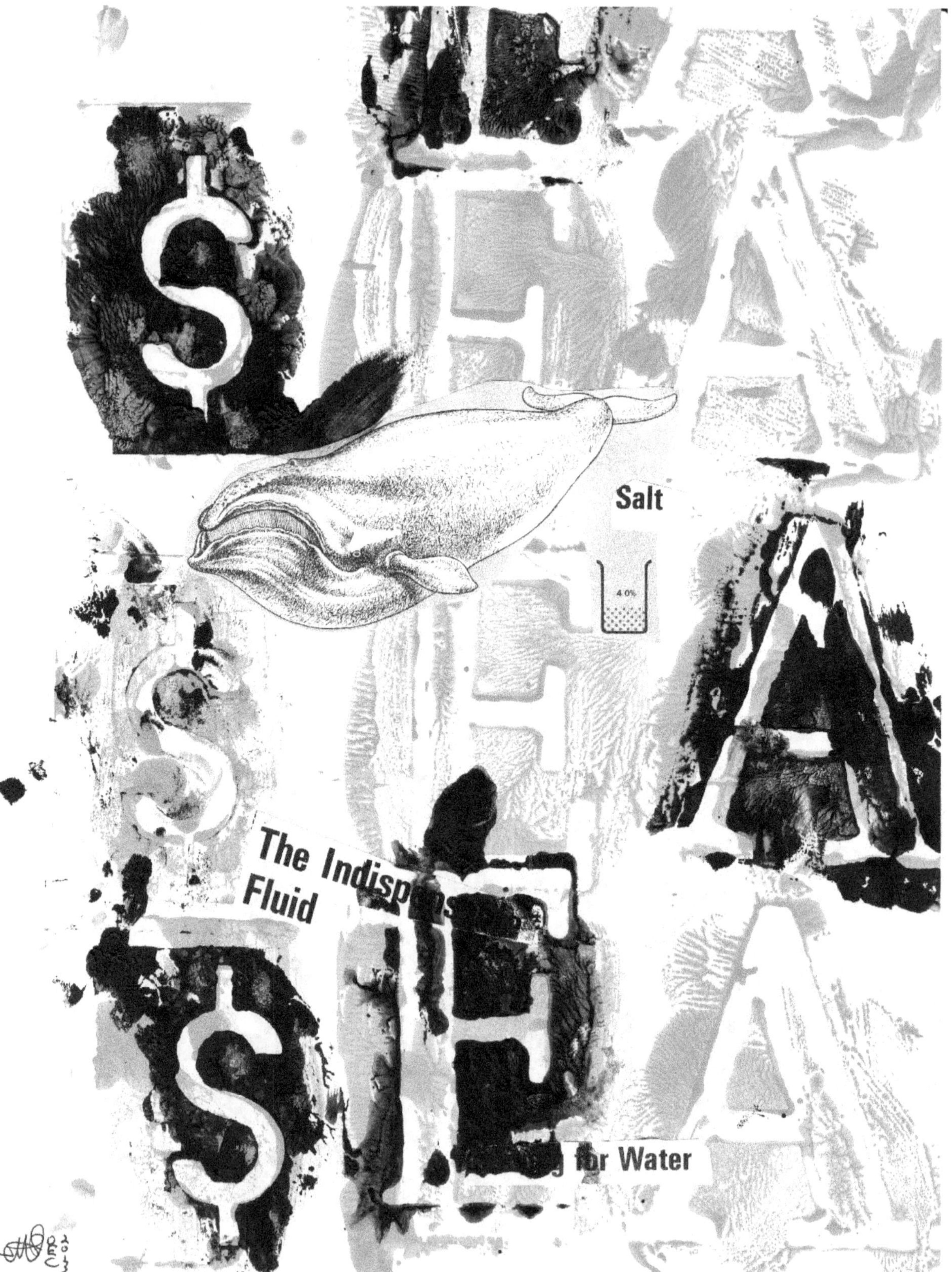
Salt
4.0%
The Indispens
Fluid
r Water

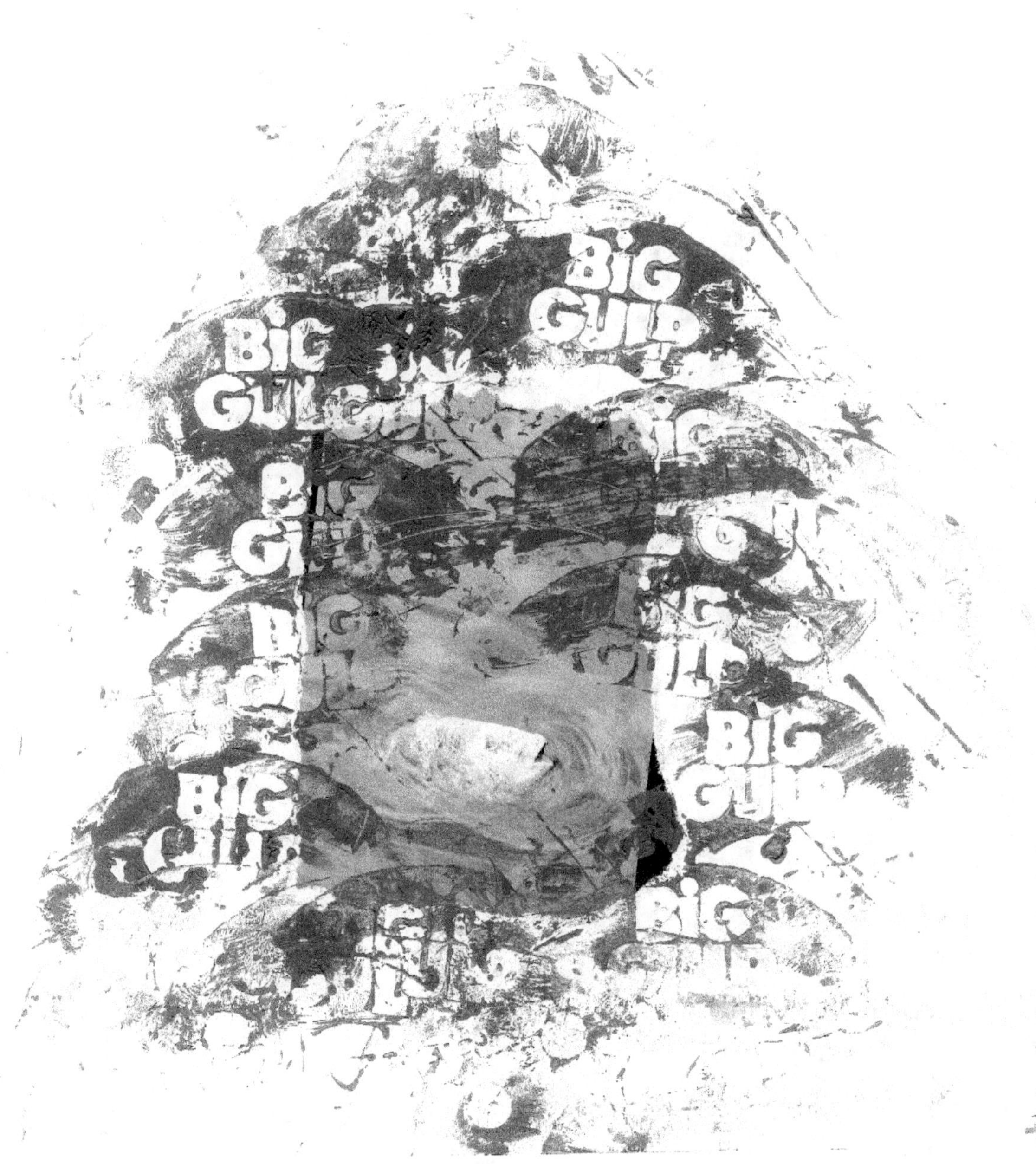
BIG
GULP

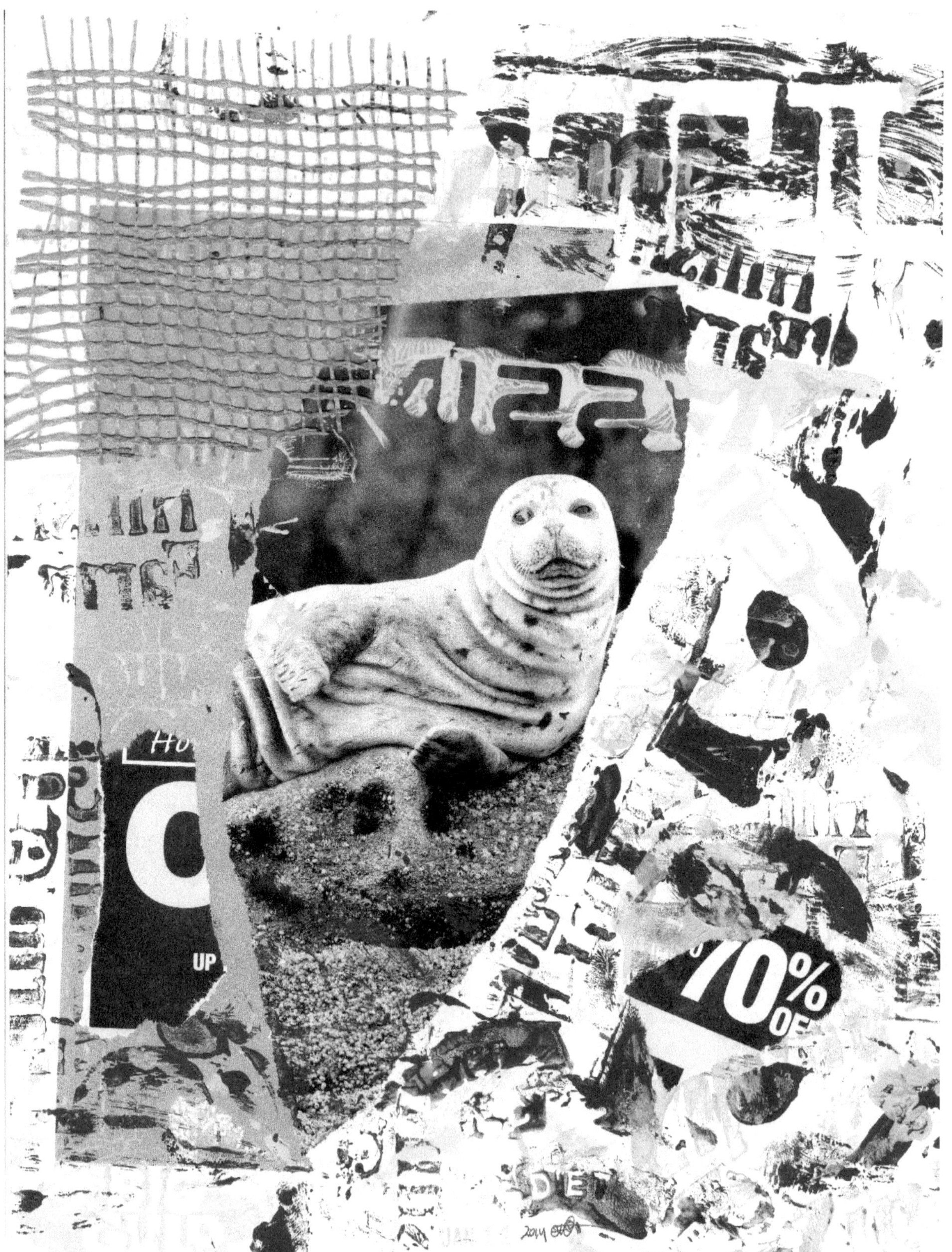
UP
70%
OF

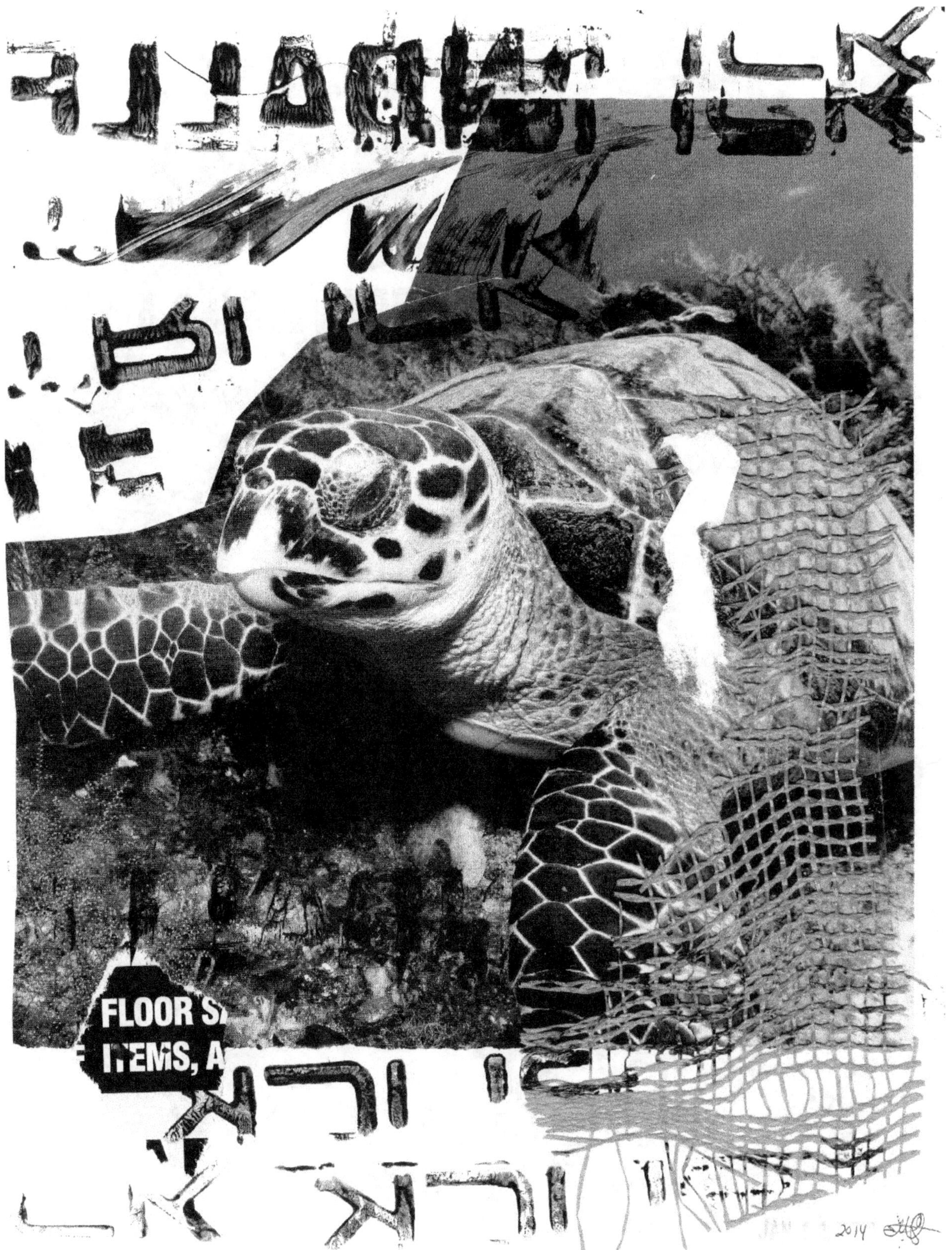
FLOOR S
ITEMS, A
2014

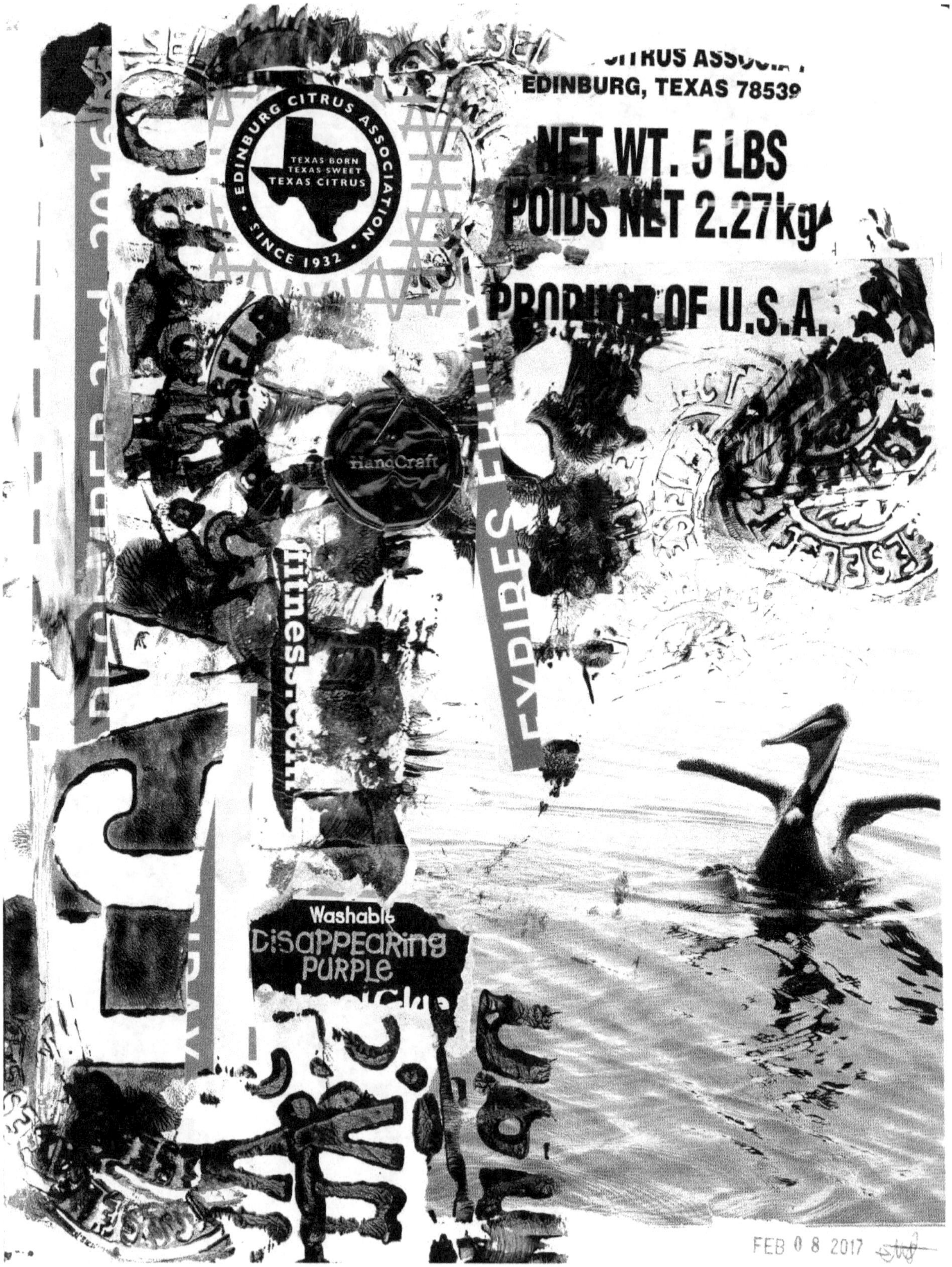

CITRUS ASSOCIA

EDINBURG, TEXAS 78539

NET WT. 5 LBS

POIDS NET 2.27kg

PRODUCE OF U.S.A.

EDINBURG CITRUS ASSOCIATION

TEXAS BORN

TEXAS SWEET

TEXAS CITRUS

SINCE 1932

HandCraft

fitness.com

EXPIRES

Washable

DisappEaRing

PURPLE

FEB 0 8 2017

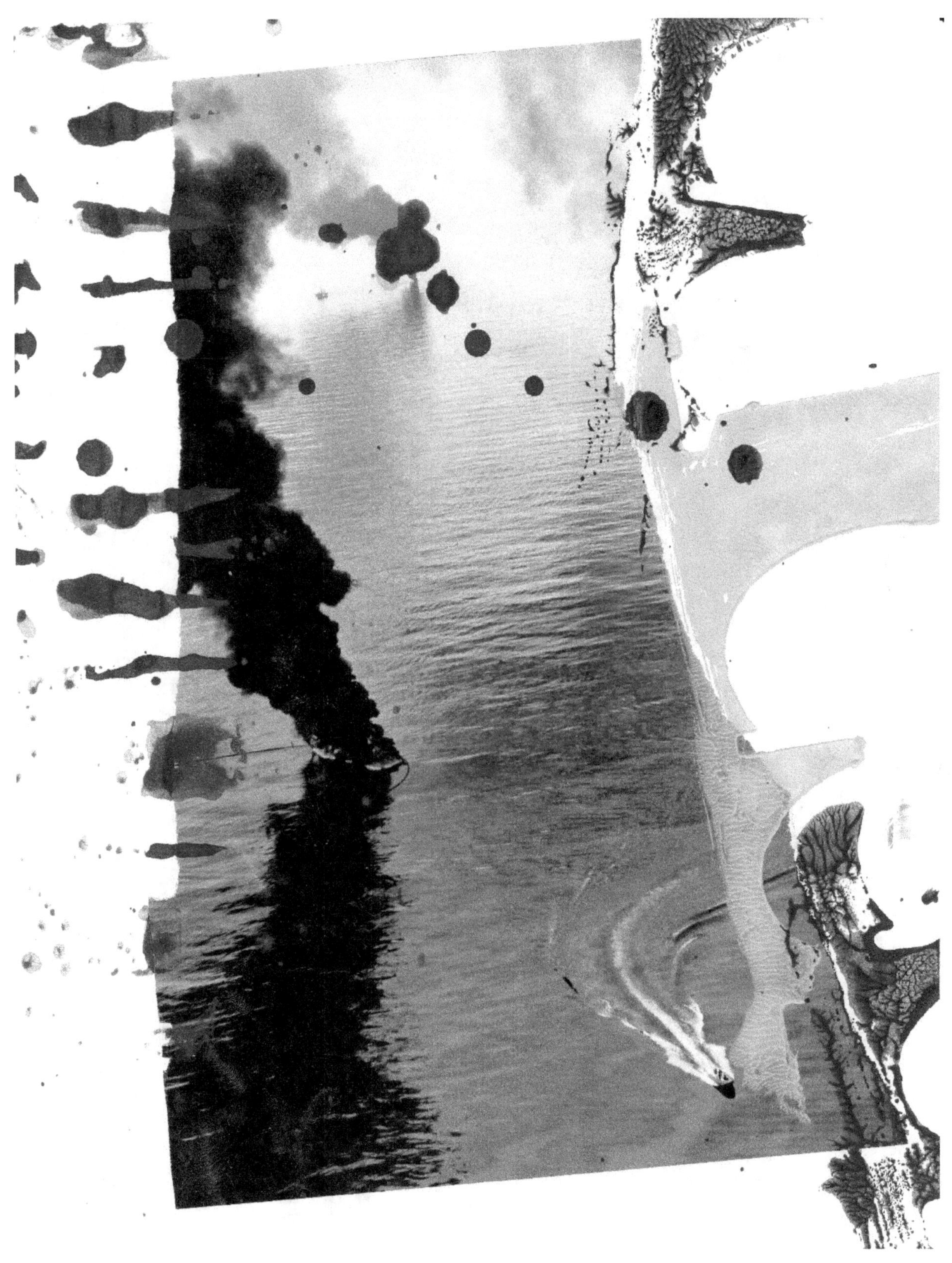

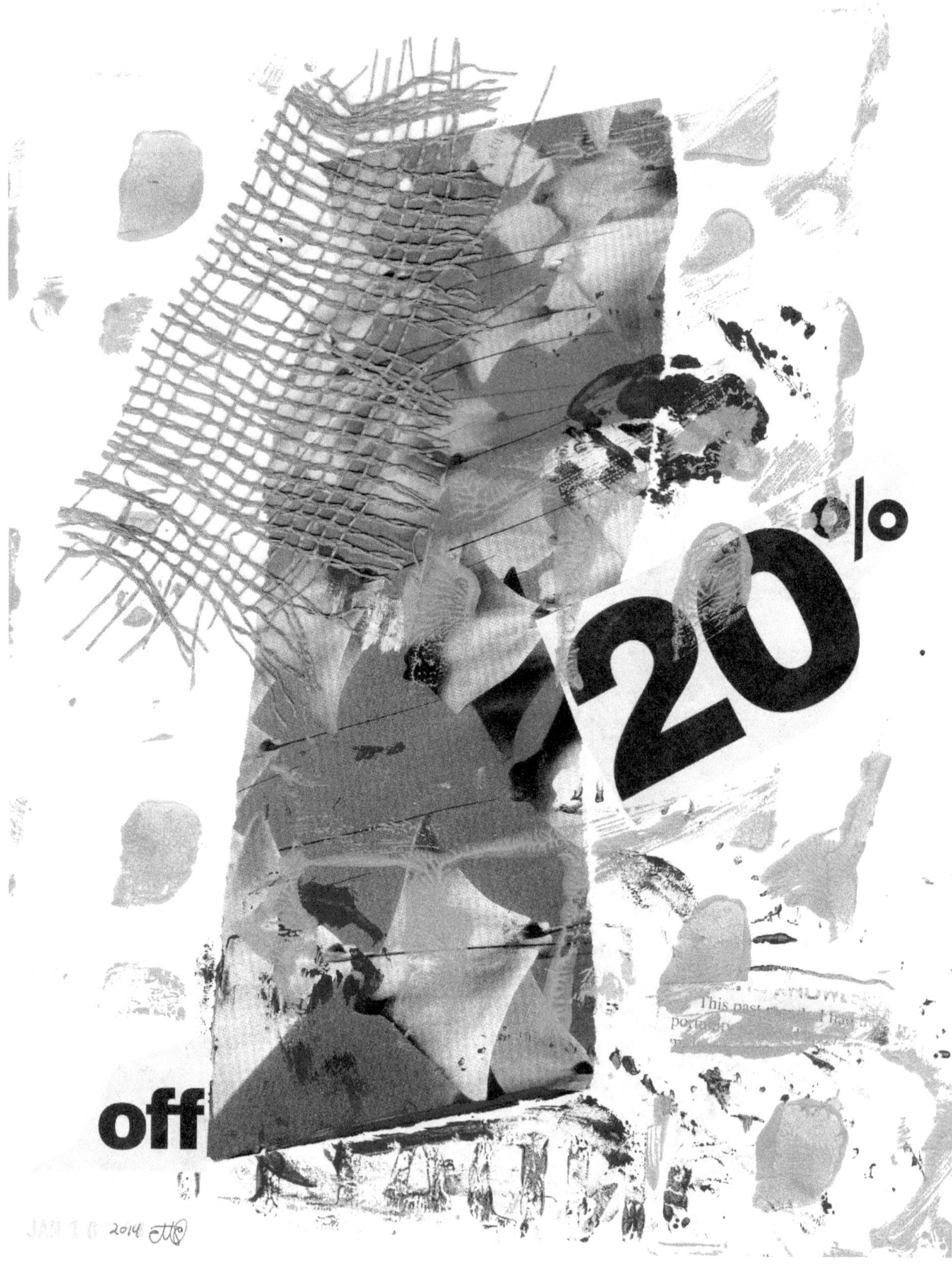
20%
off
This past
2014

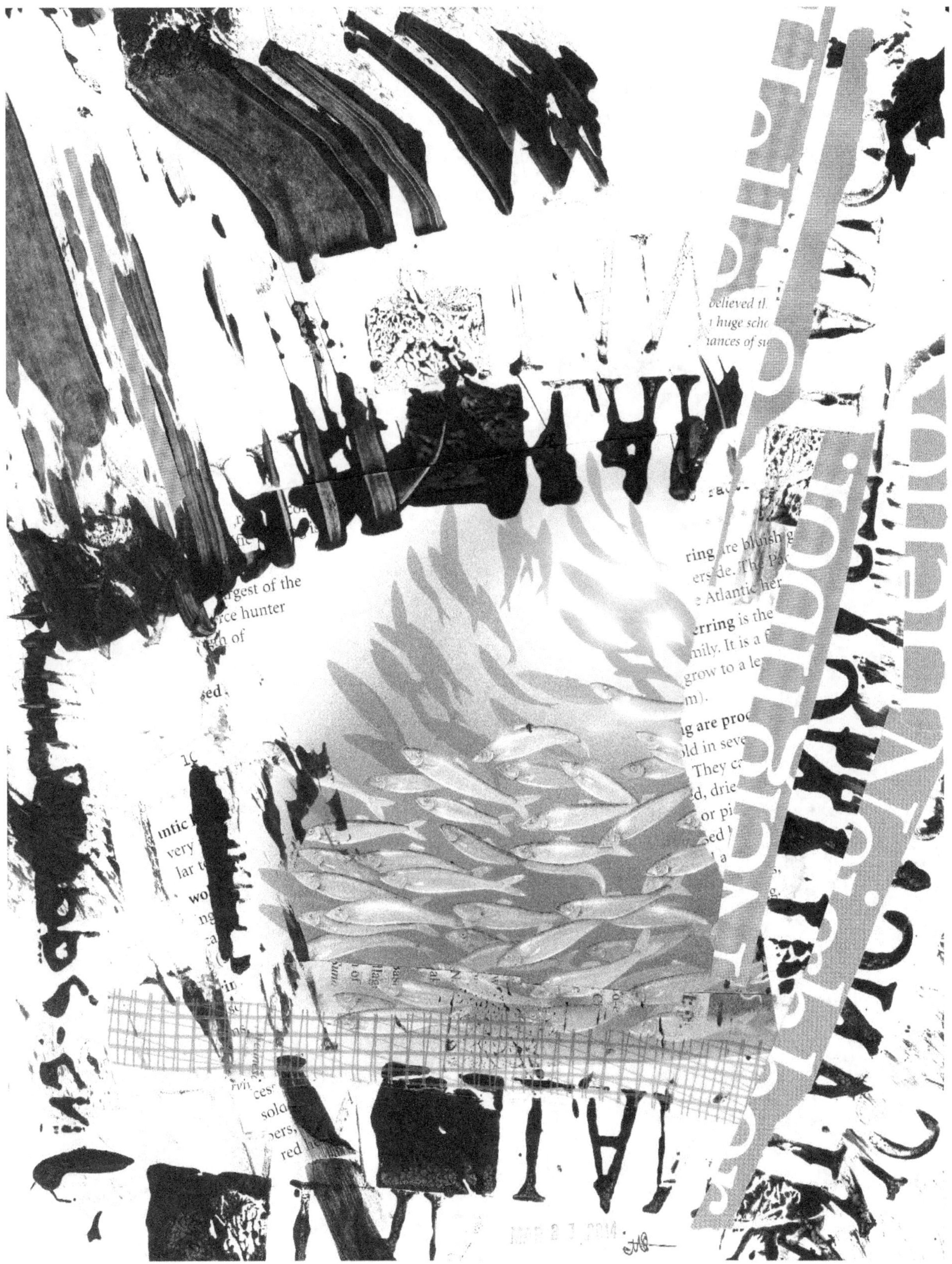

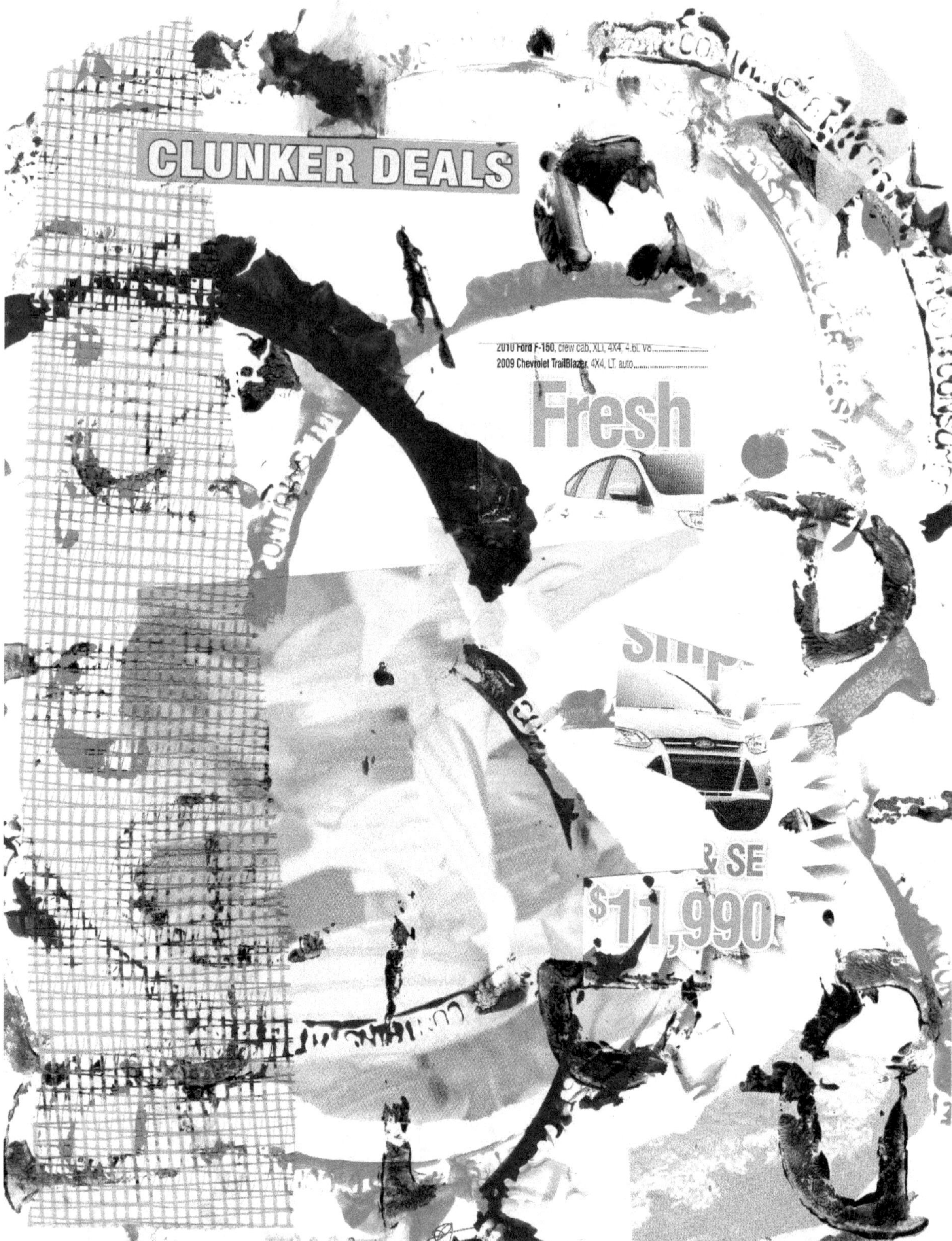
CLUNKER DEALS
2010 Ford F-150, crew cab, XLT, 4X4, 4.6L V8
2009 Chevrolet TrailBlazer, 4X4, LT, auto
Fresh
& SE
$11,990

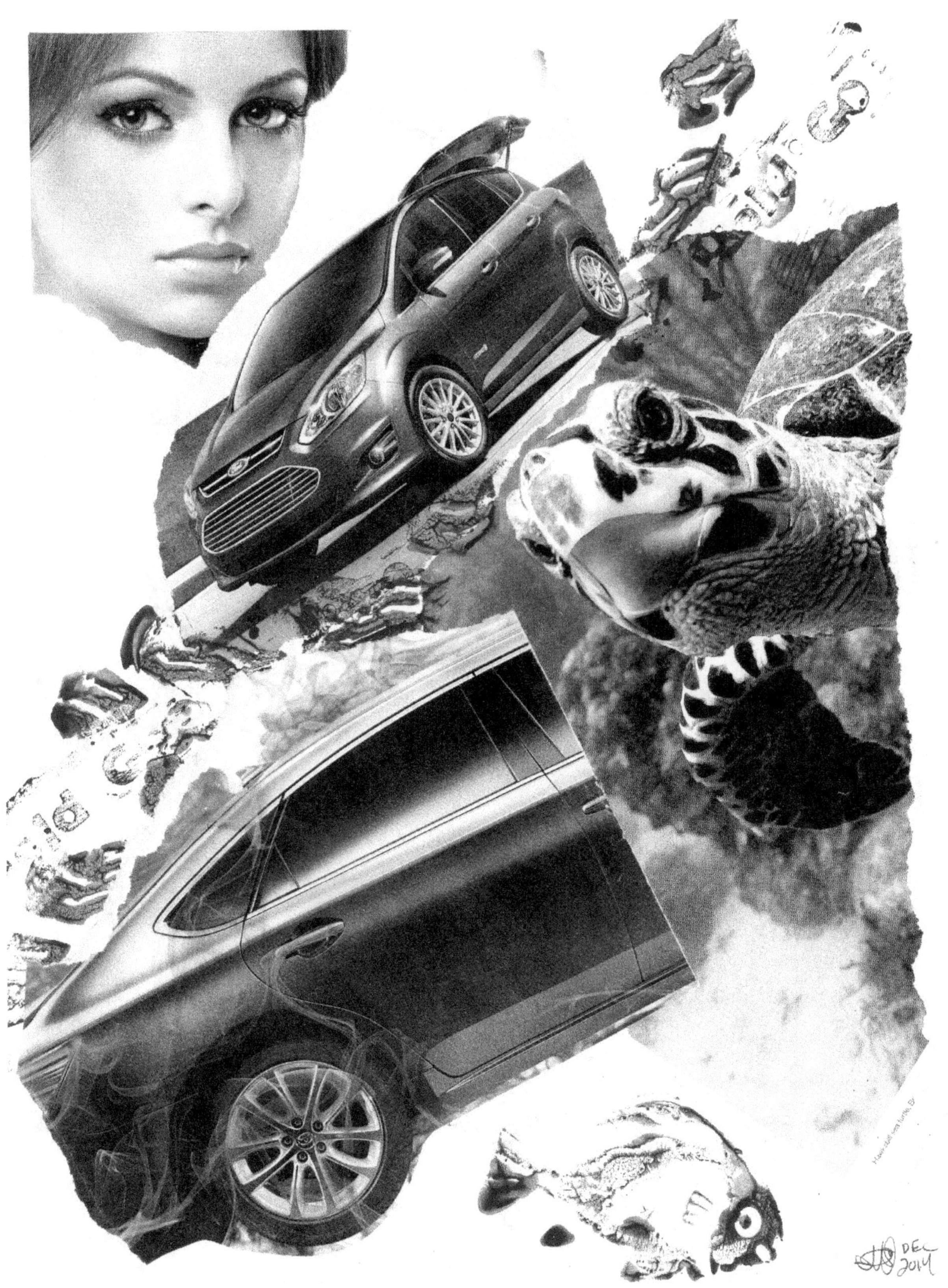
DEC
2014

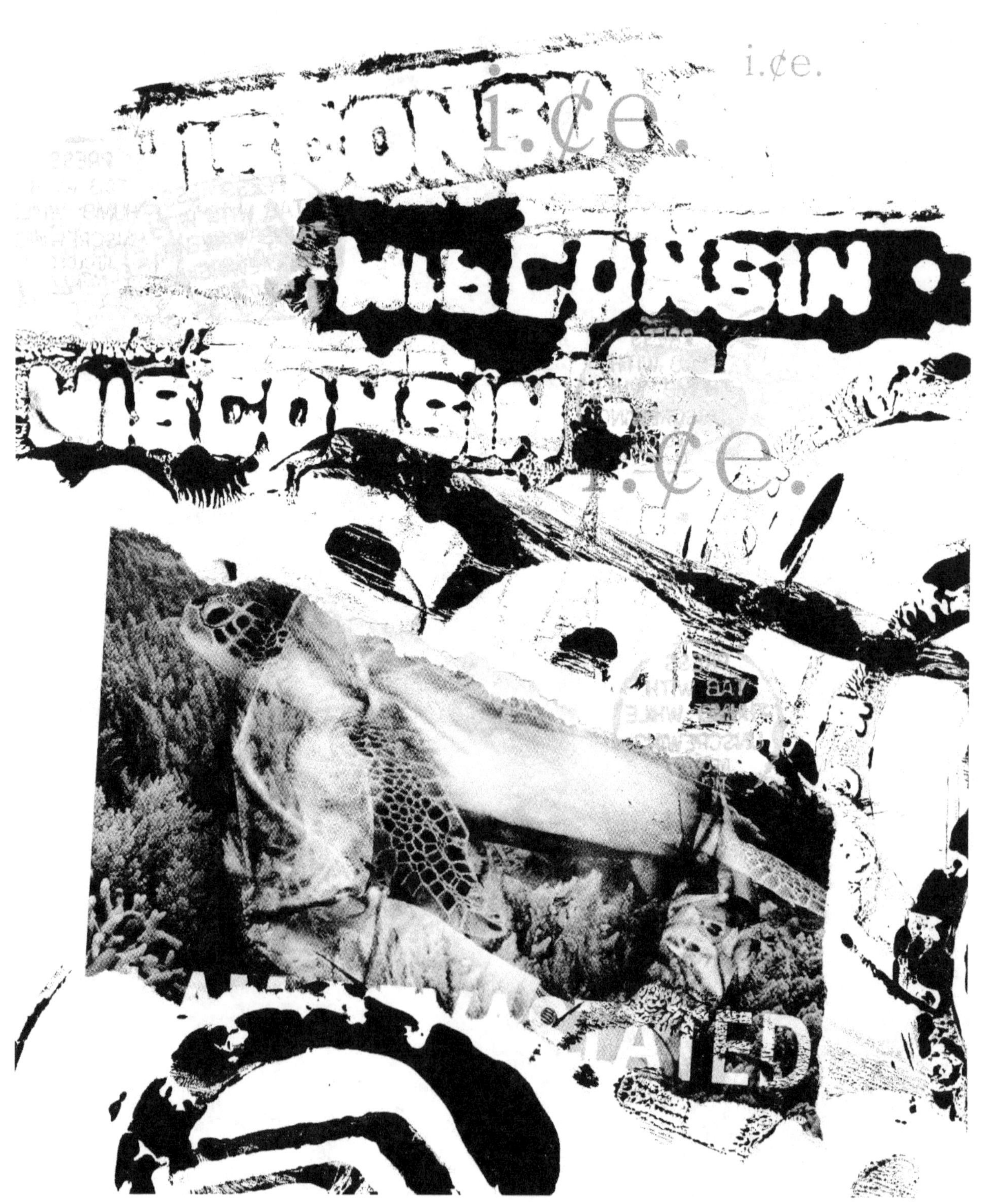
i.¢e.
i.¢e.
WISCONSIN
WISCONSIN
i.¢e.

balance

life

APR 0 6 2014

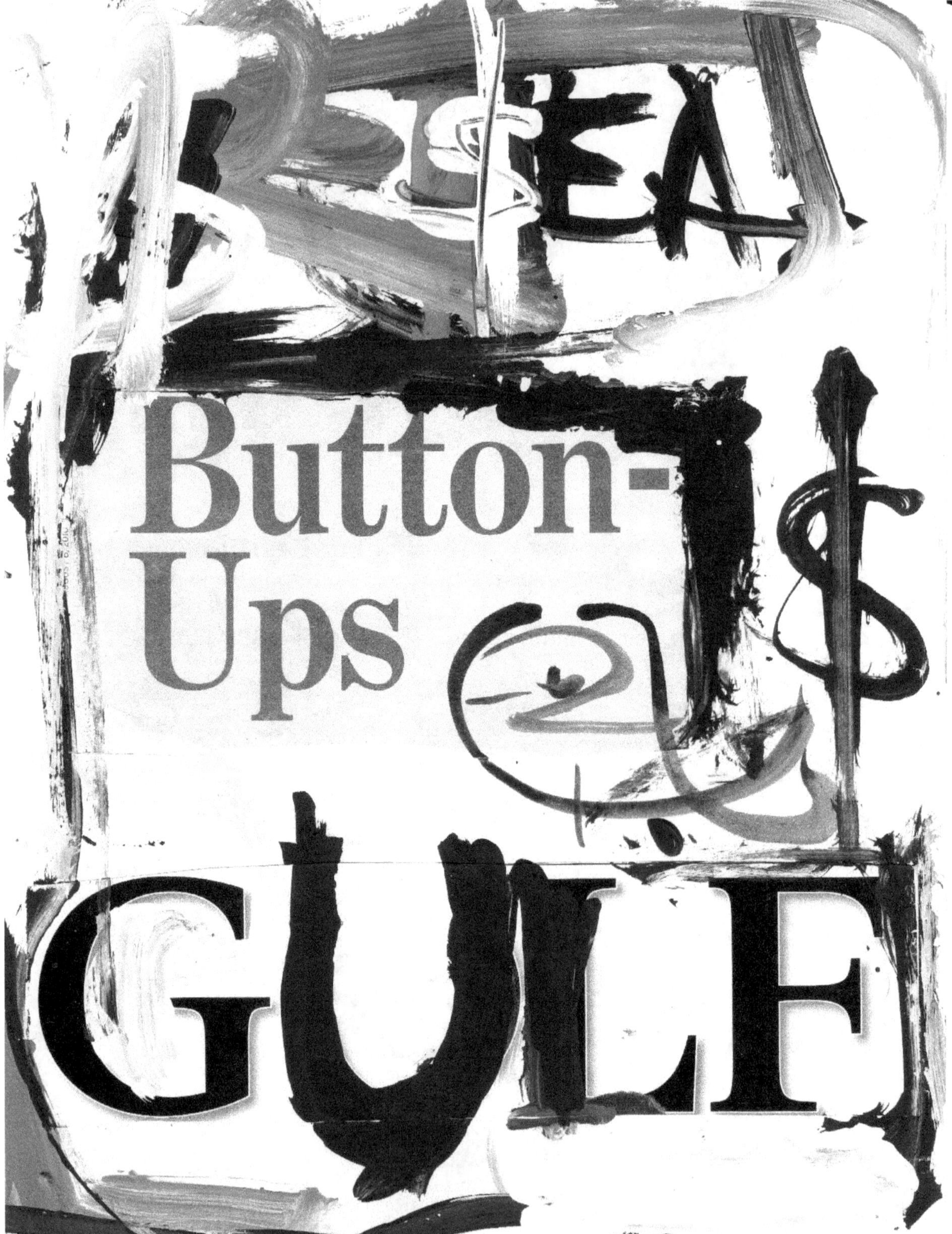
Button-
Ups
GULF

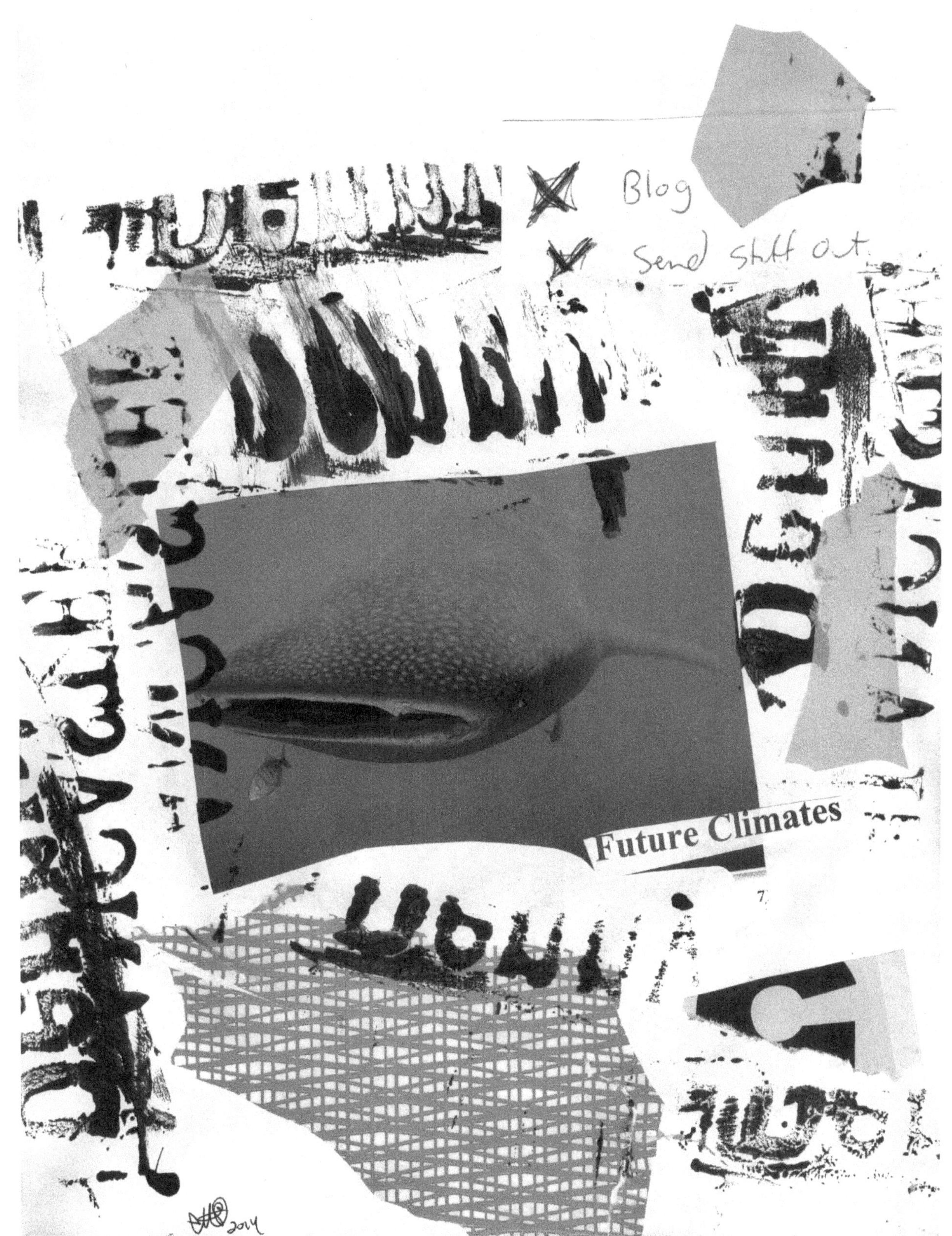

Blog
Send Stuff Out
Future Climates
7
2014

LAST

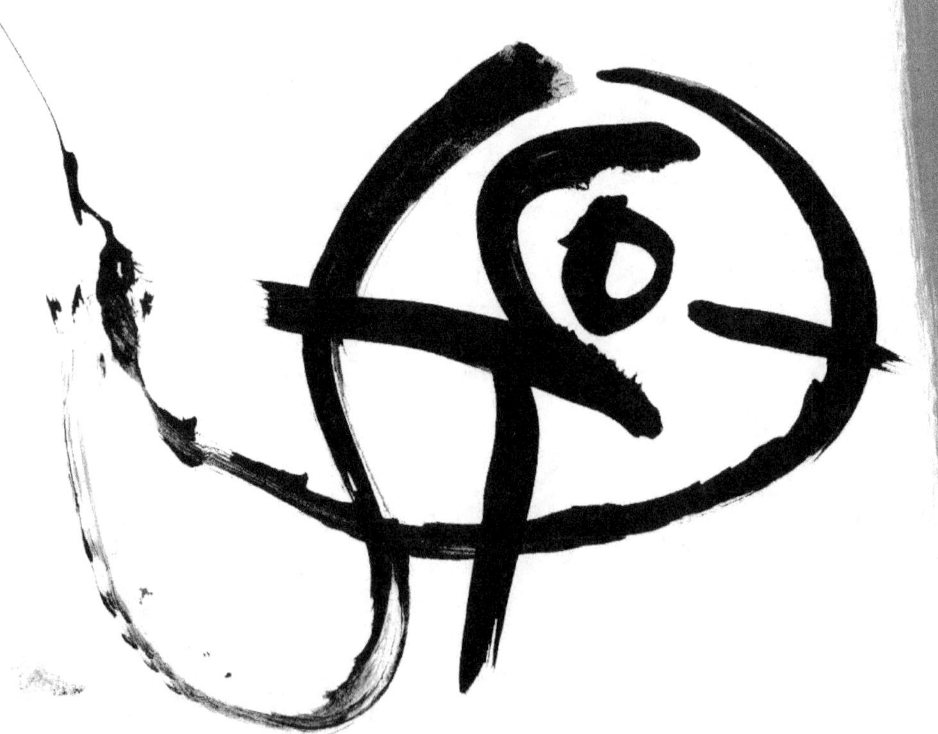

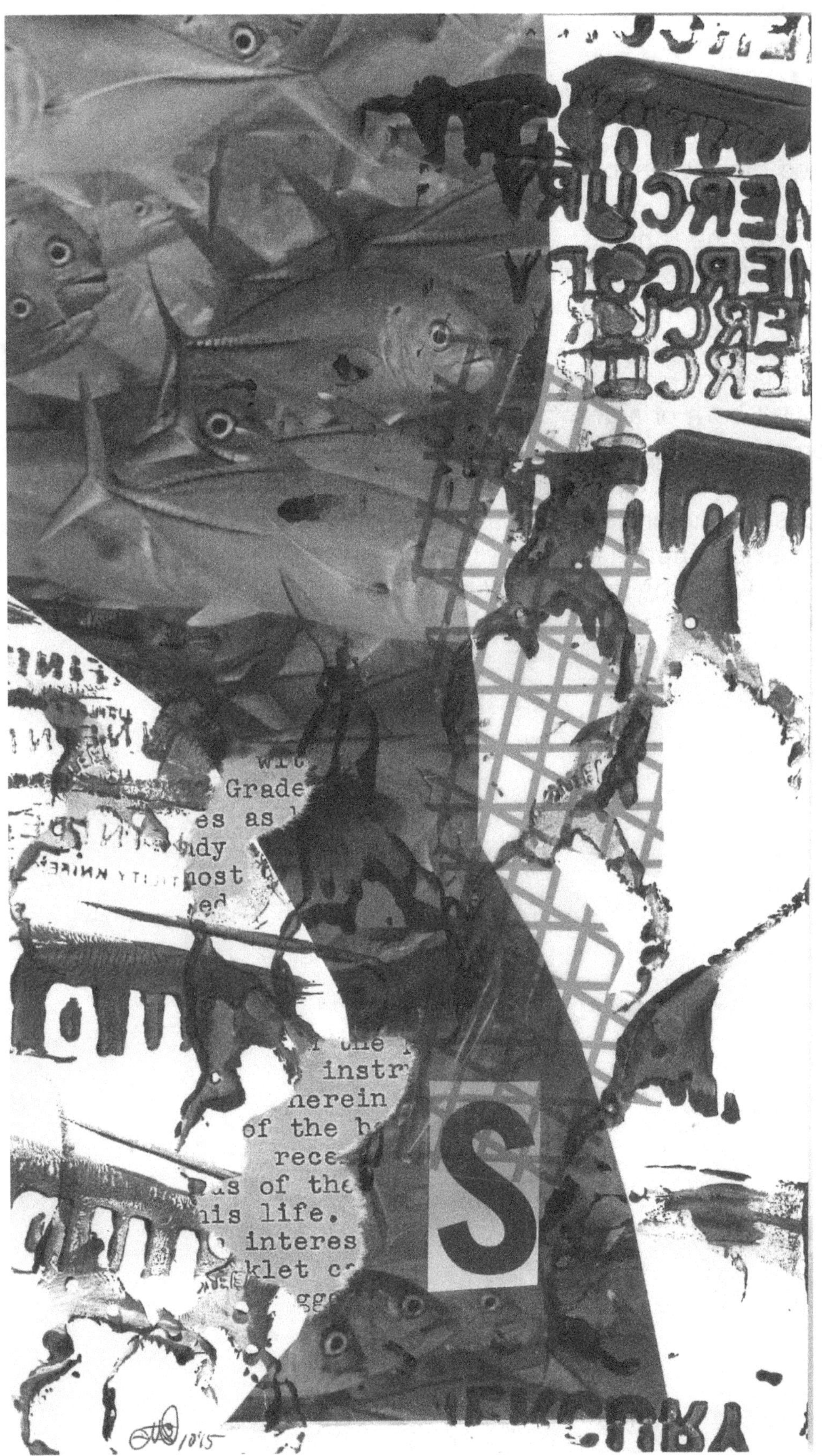
MERCURY
Grade
es as
most
instr
herein
of the
rece
of the
is life.
interes
klet c

5

Collaborations

In 2019 I initiated more collaborations with Andrew Topel – black & white, 8 ½ x 11, all exchanged through the mail. We made about 100 works. Andrew sent them all back to me & published a chapbook in 2020 under his avantacular press, titled *Language Mangler*. I planned on reciprocating by publishing a chapbook of my own, titled *Manguage Langler*, but I never got around to it what with COVID-19. I chose works not published in *Language Mangler* for this collection.

This book was born of a grant proposal. I needed a letter of recommendation so I asked C. Mehrl Bennett. She responded immediately with a generous letter. I thought I may as well ask her if she'd like to make new collaborations for the project. She agreed, so I roped in John M. Bennett, thinking I had unpublished collaborations & paintings to include from both of them. To my delight, C. Mehrl Bennett offered to make the cover for the book as well.

Collaborations with Andrew Topel

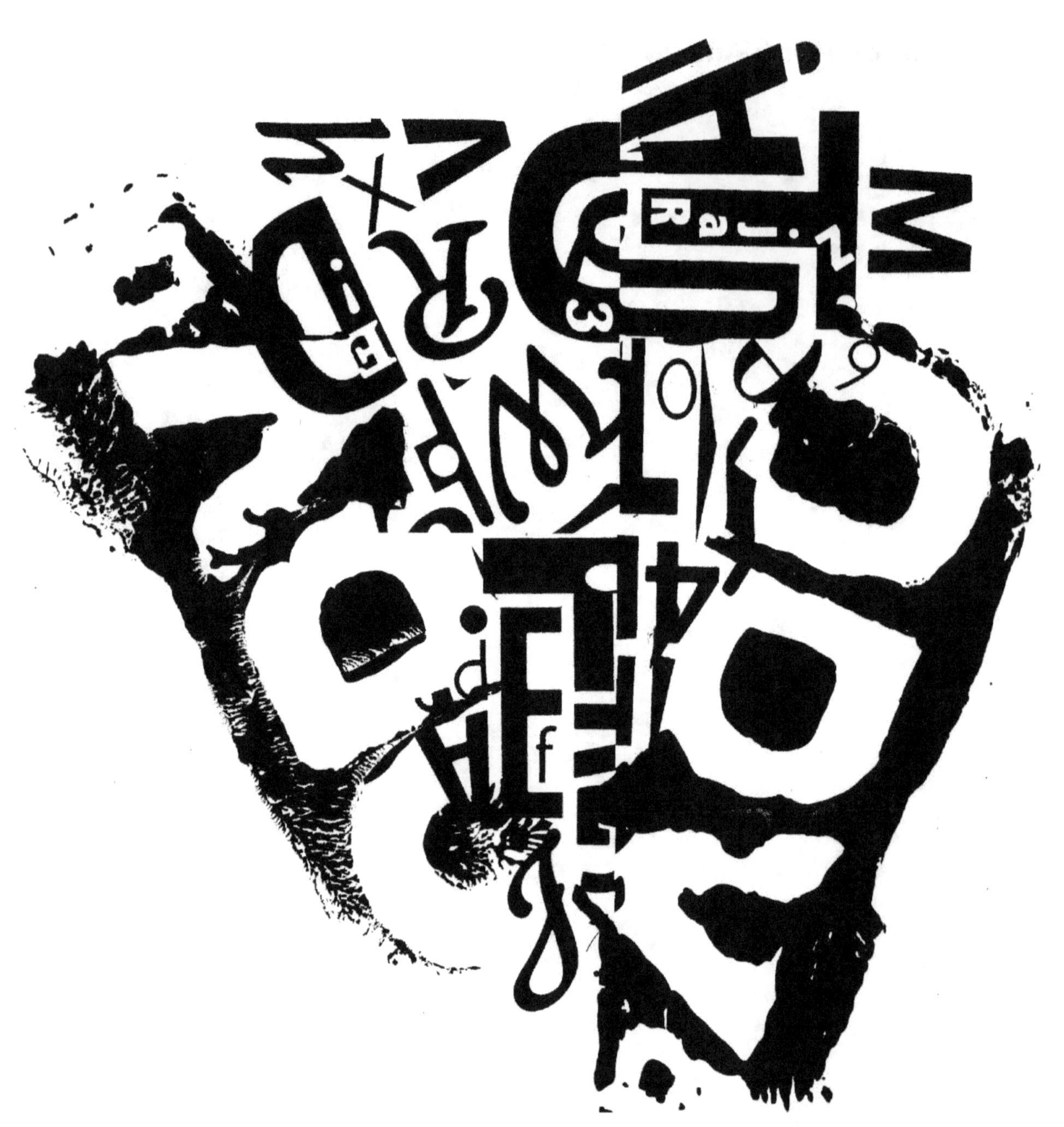

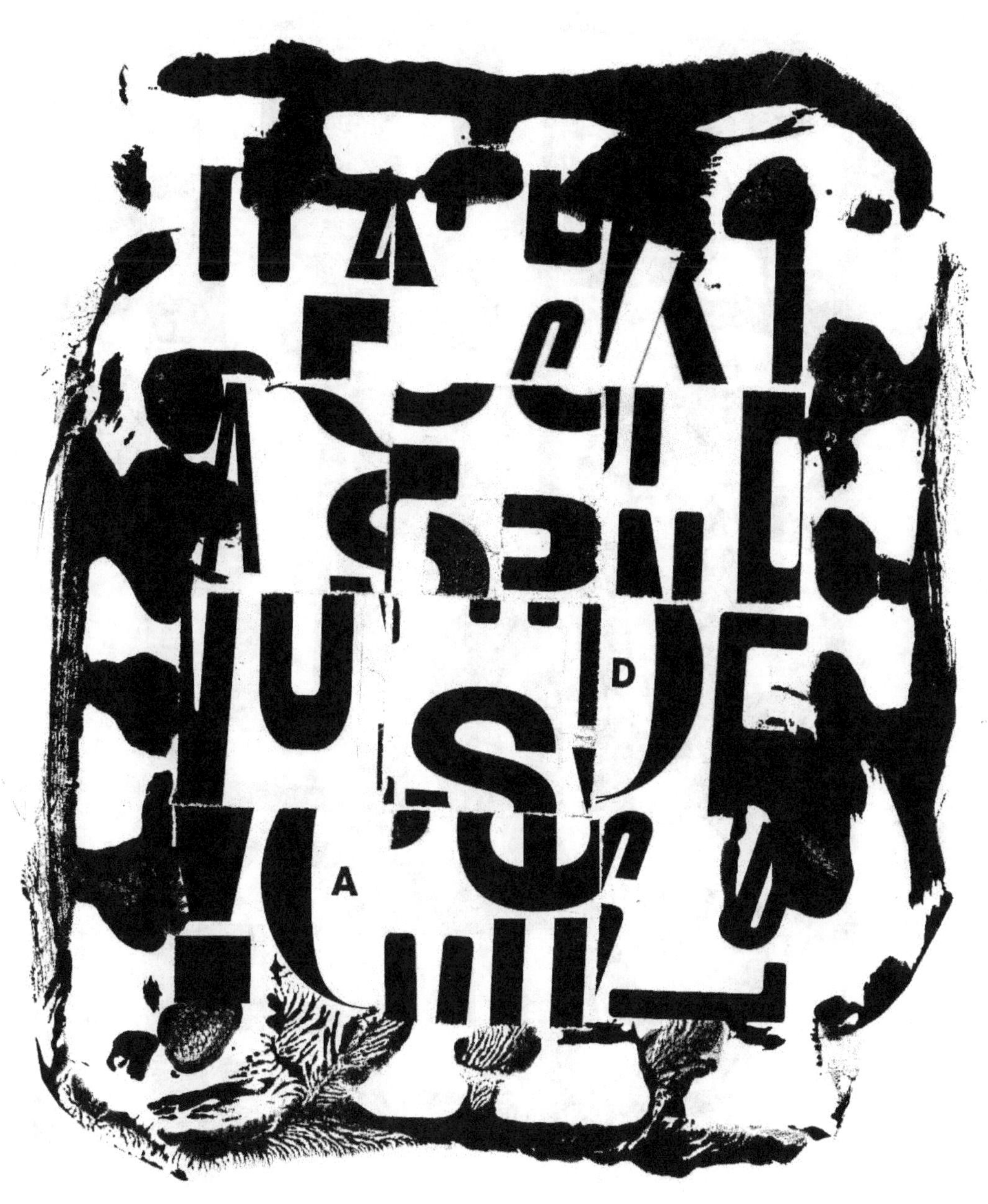

NOV 1 2 2019

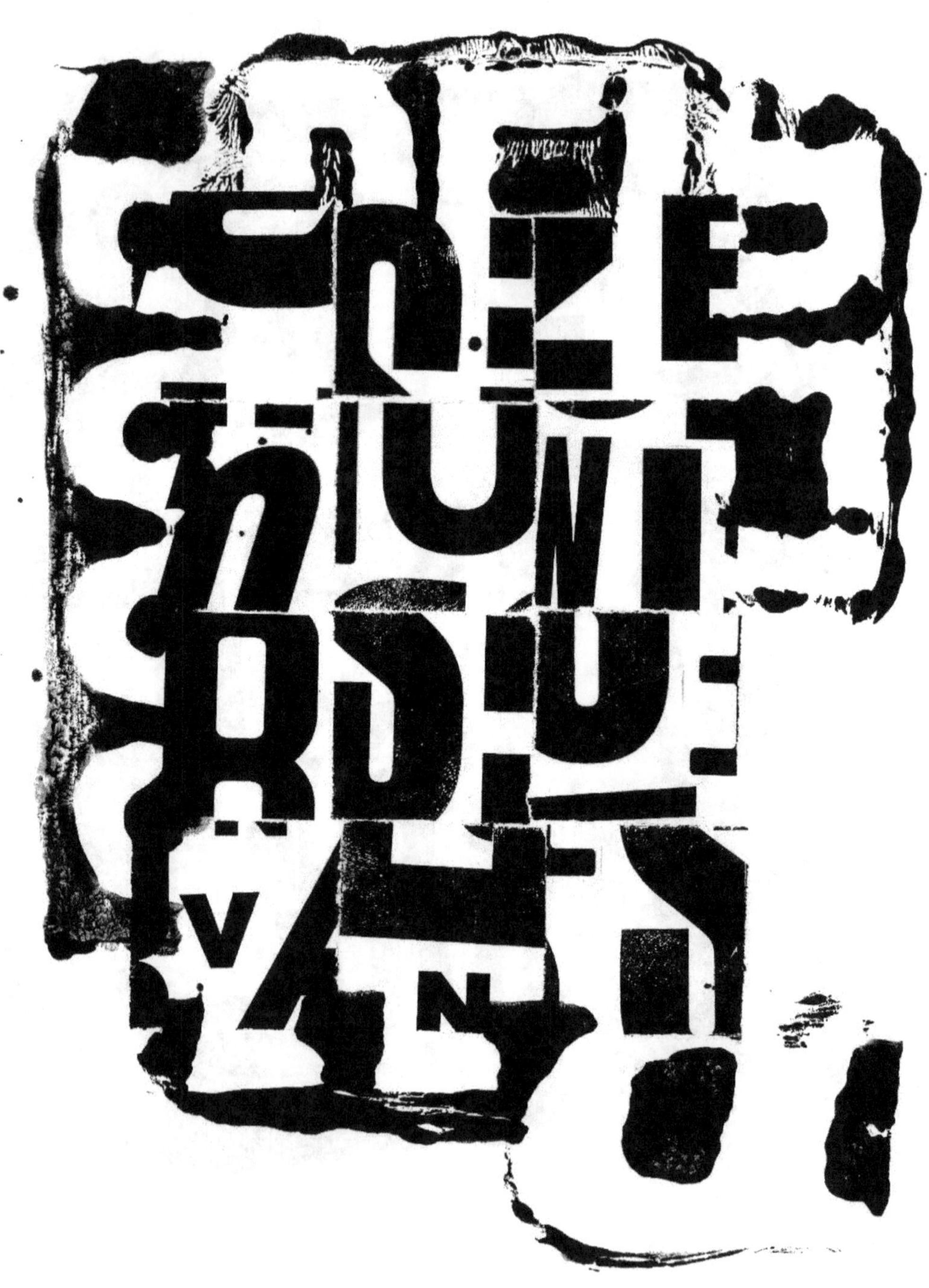

NOV 1 2 2019

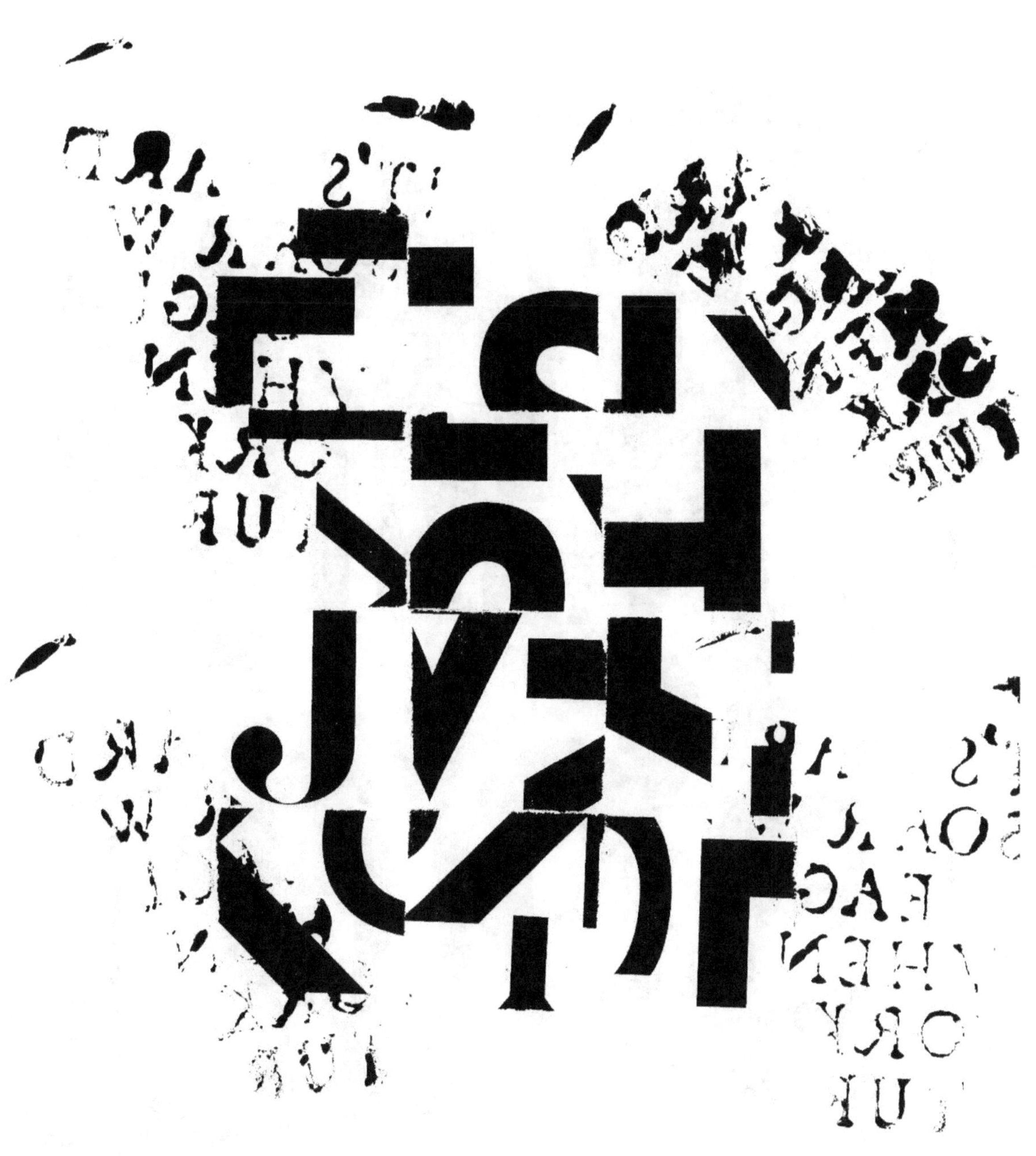

NOV 1 0 2019

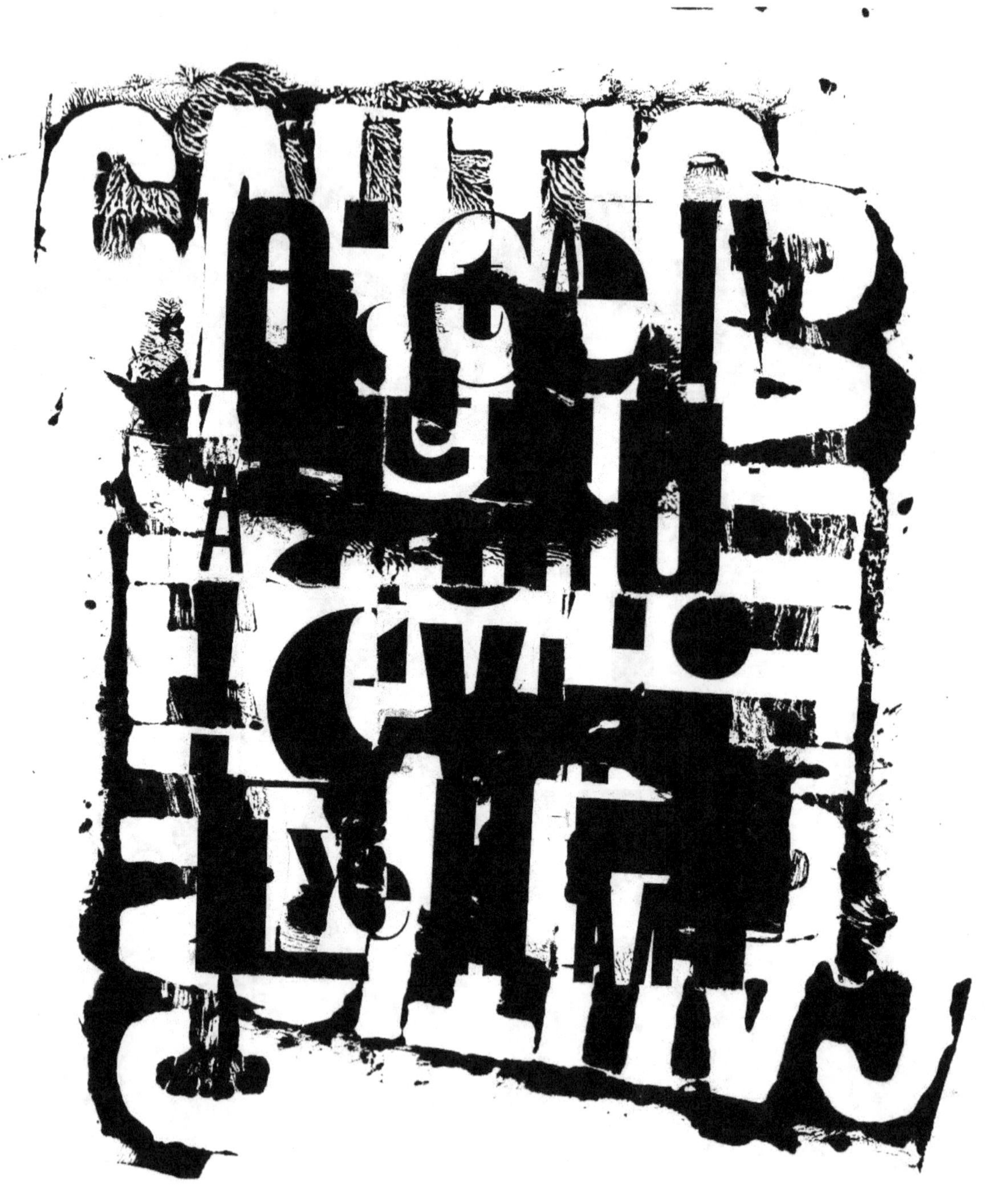

NOV 1 2 2019

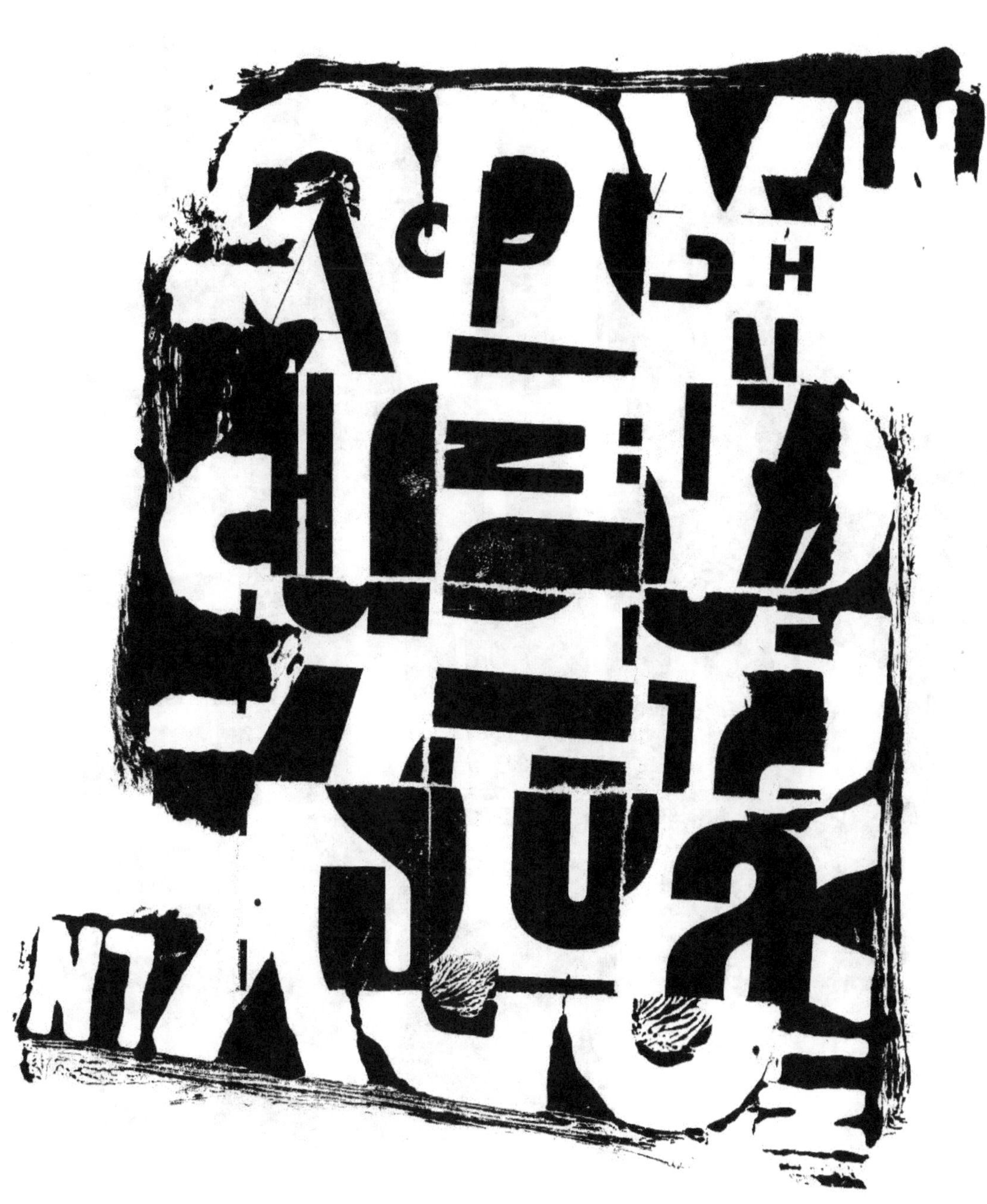

NOV 1 2 2019

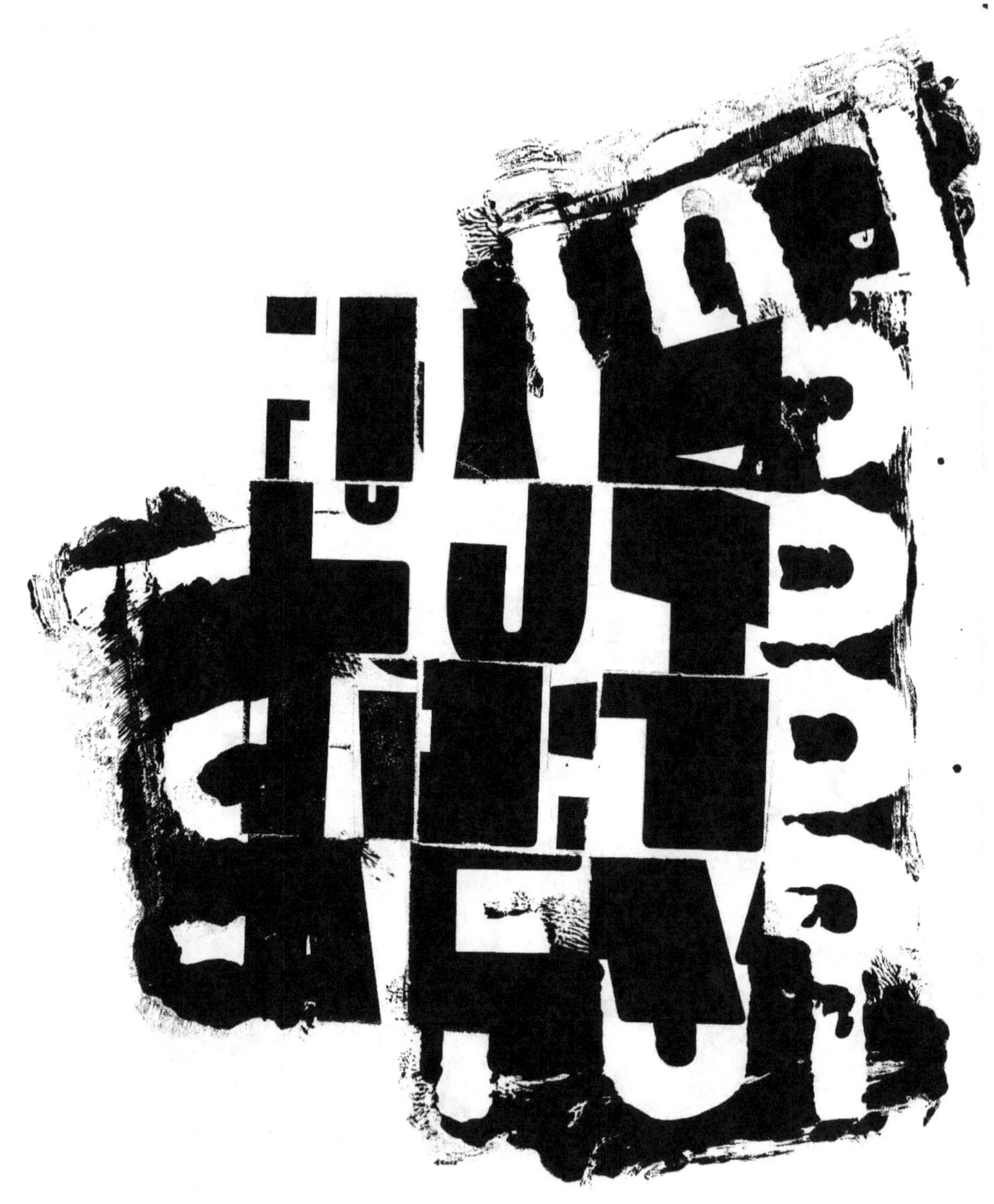

NOV 1 2 2019

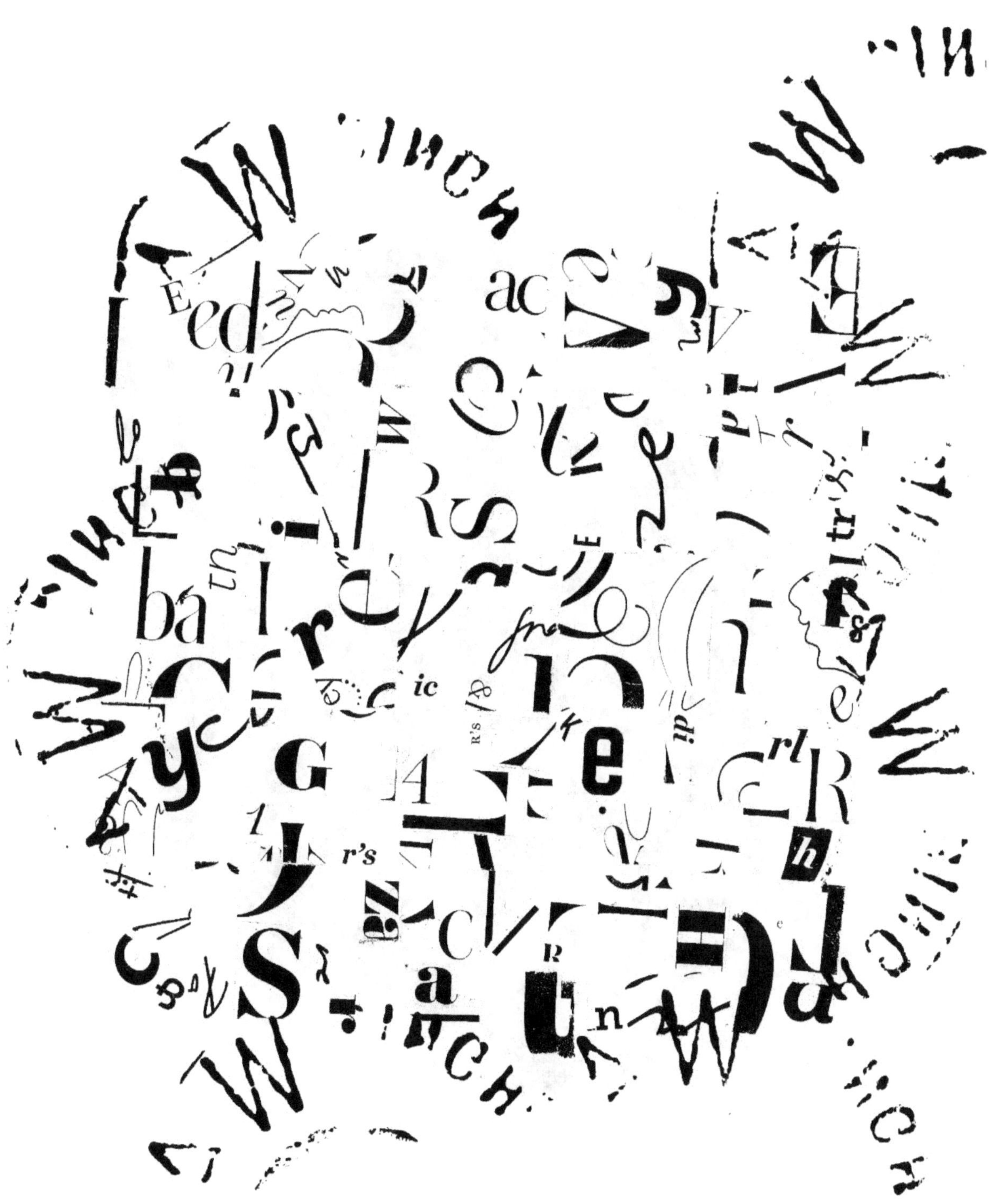
NOV 1 0 2019

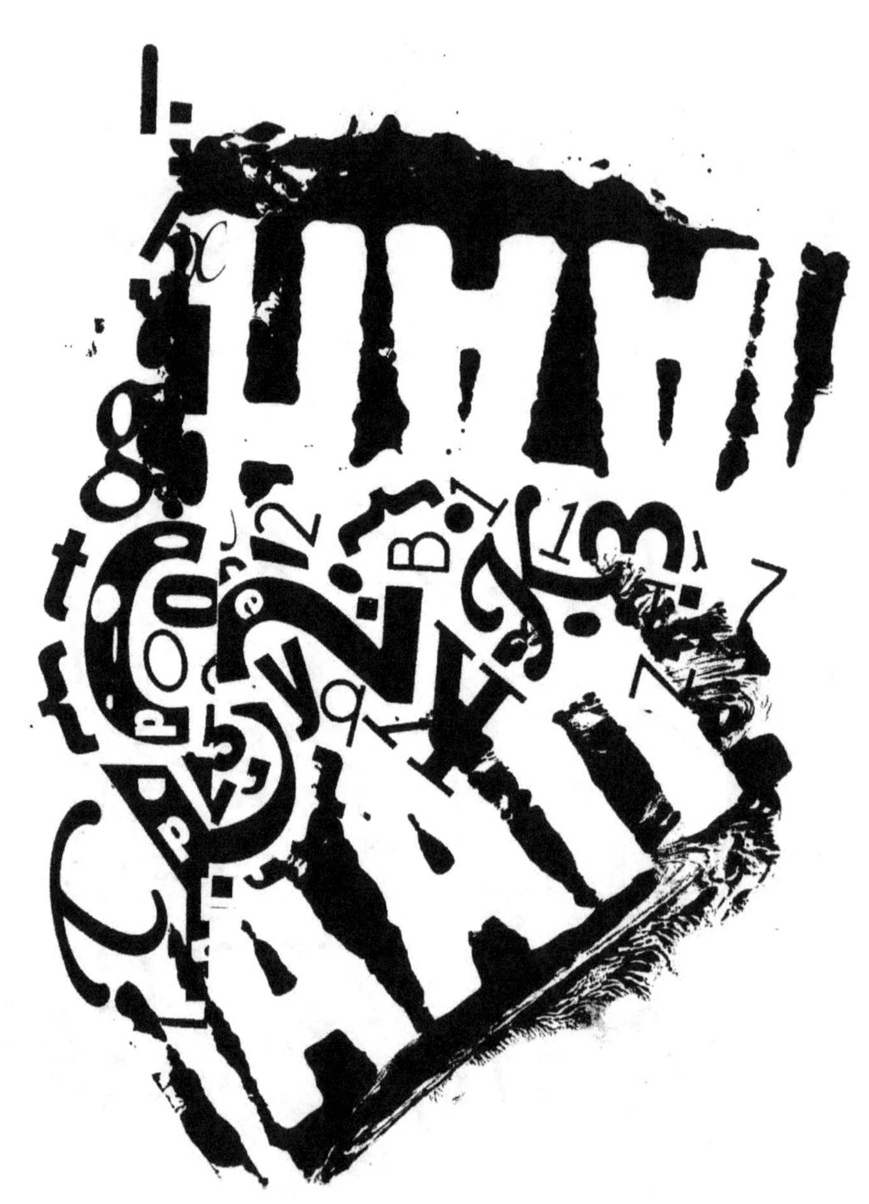

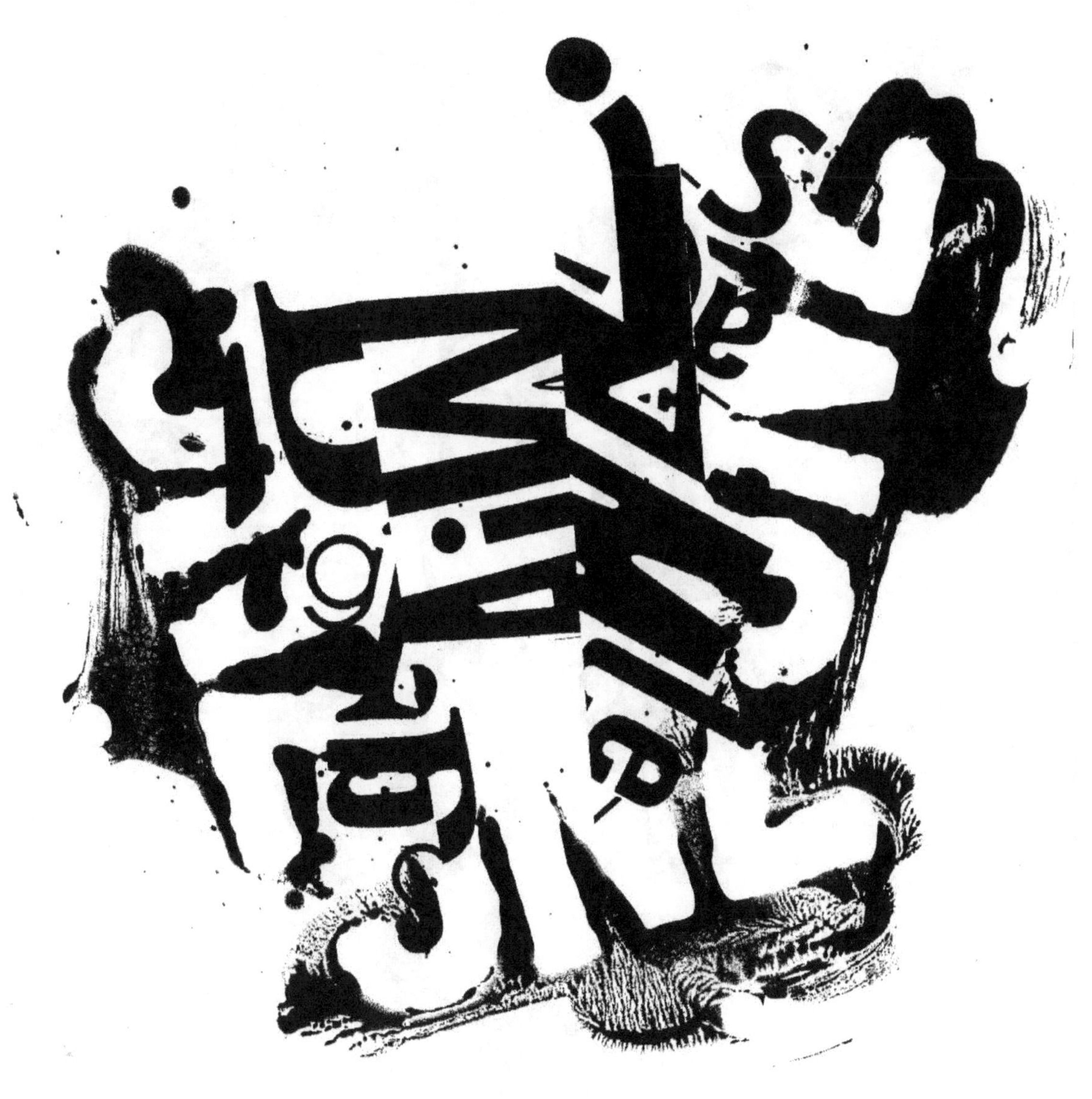

NOV 0 6 2019 A. Topel

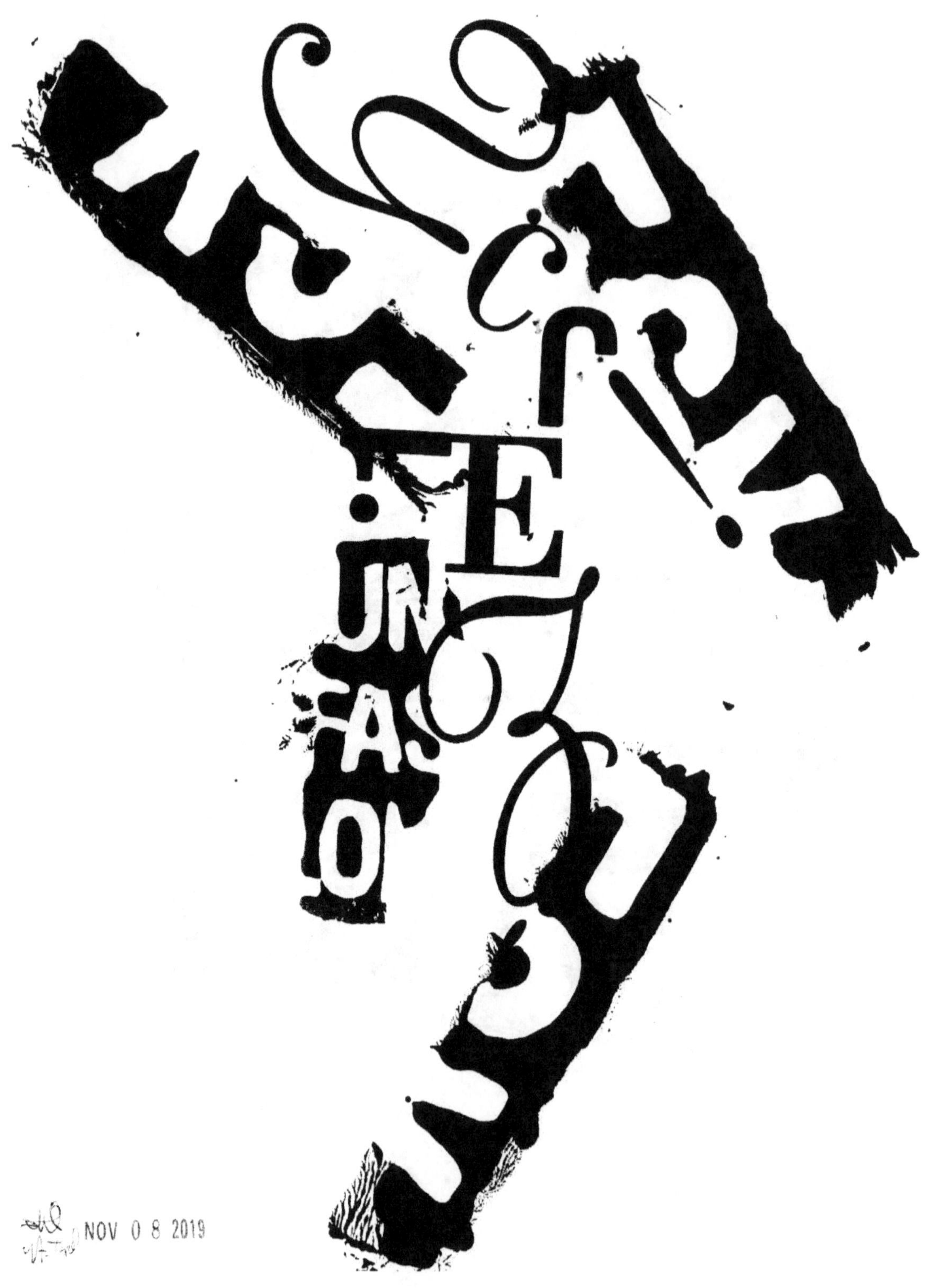

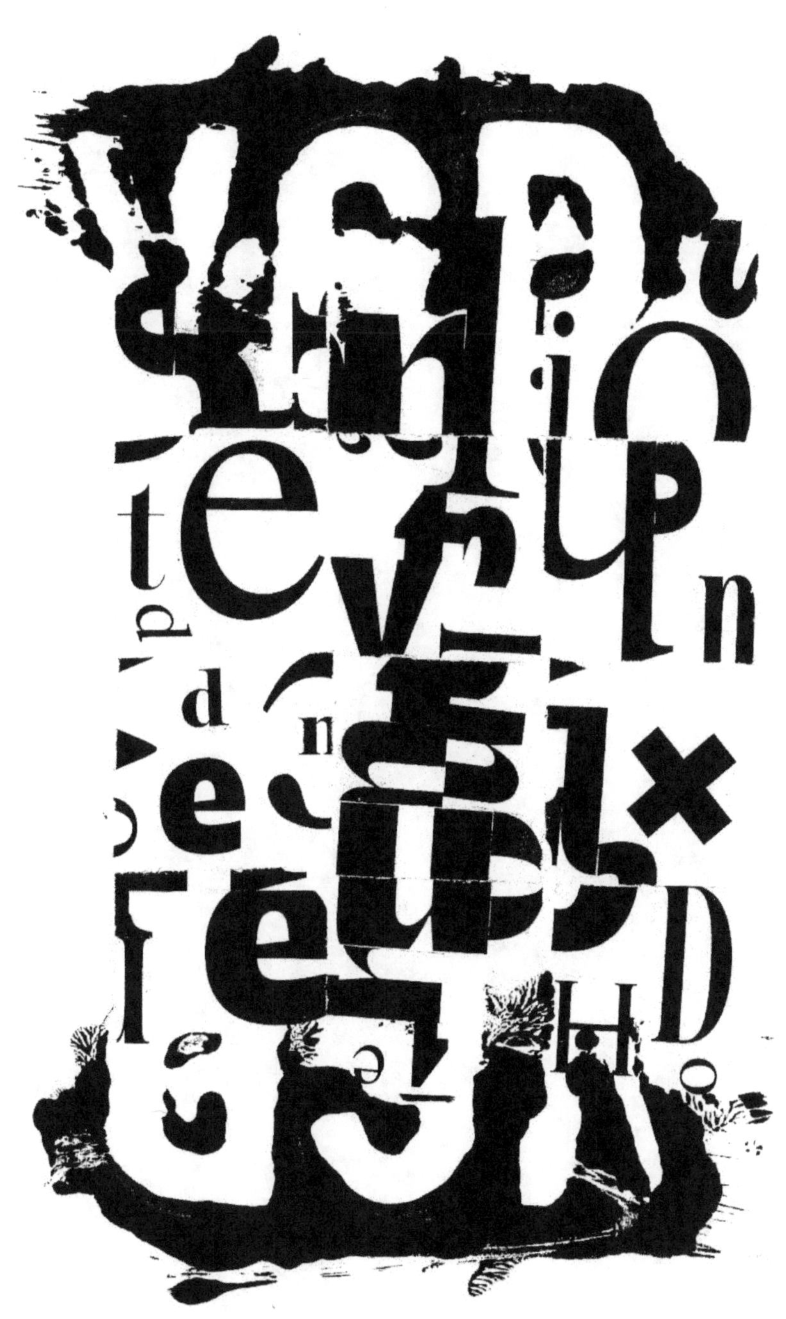

Collaborations with C. Mehrl Bennett

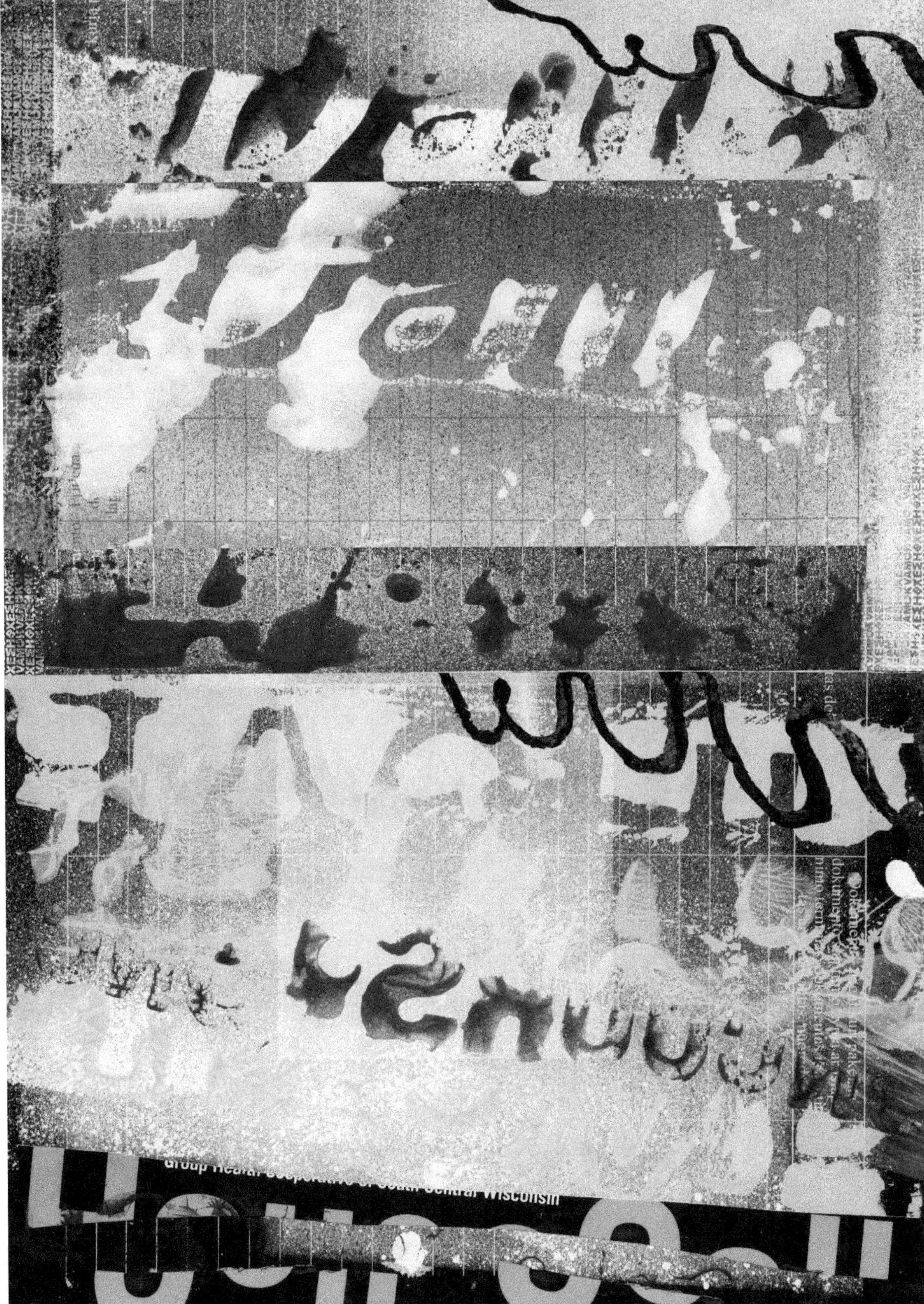

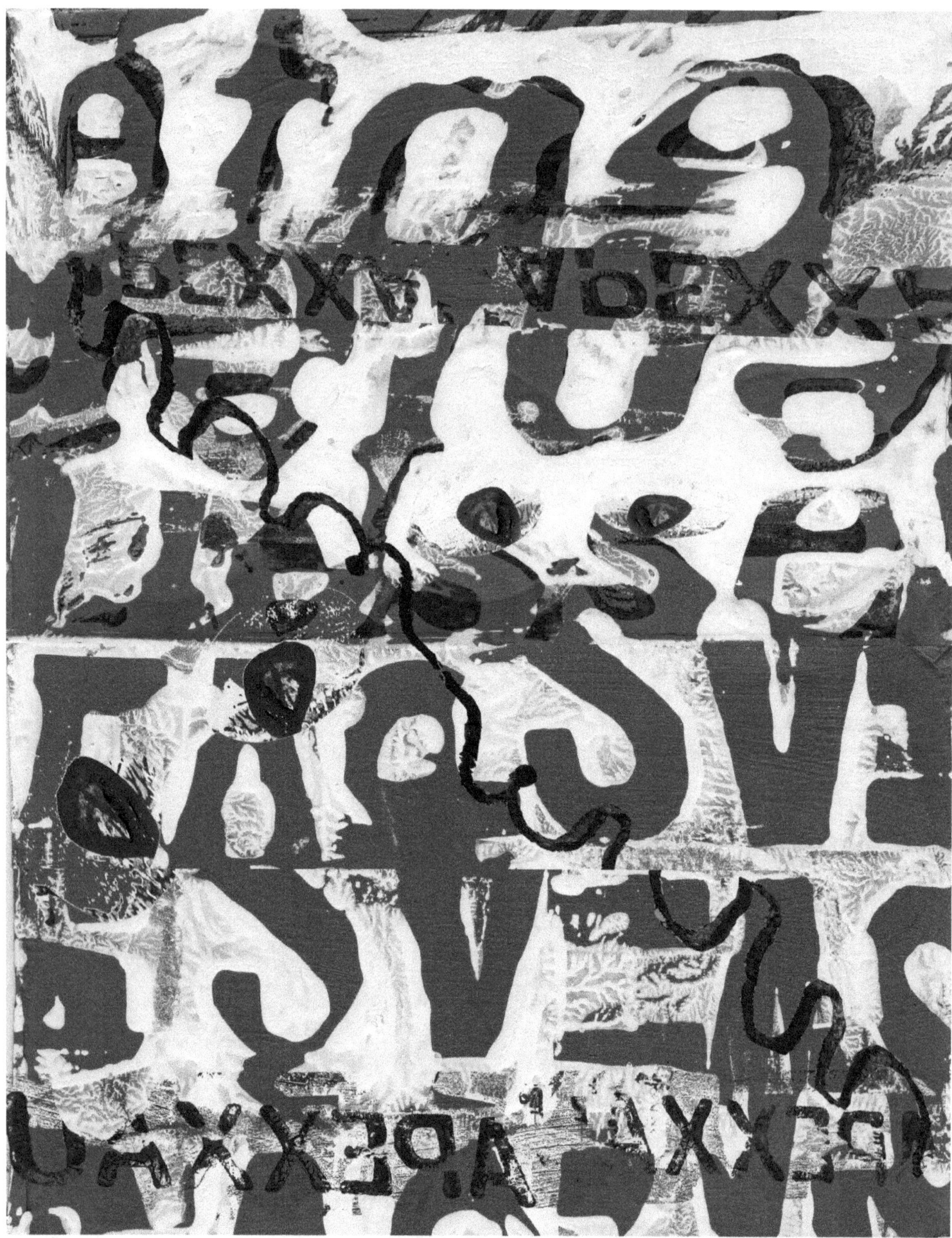

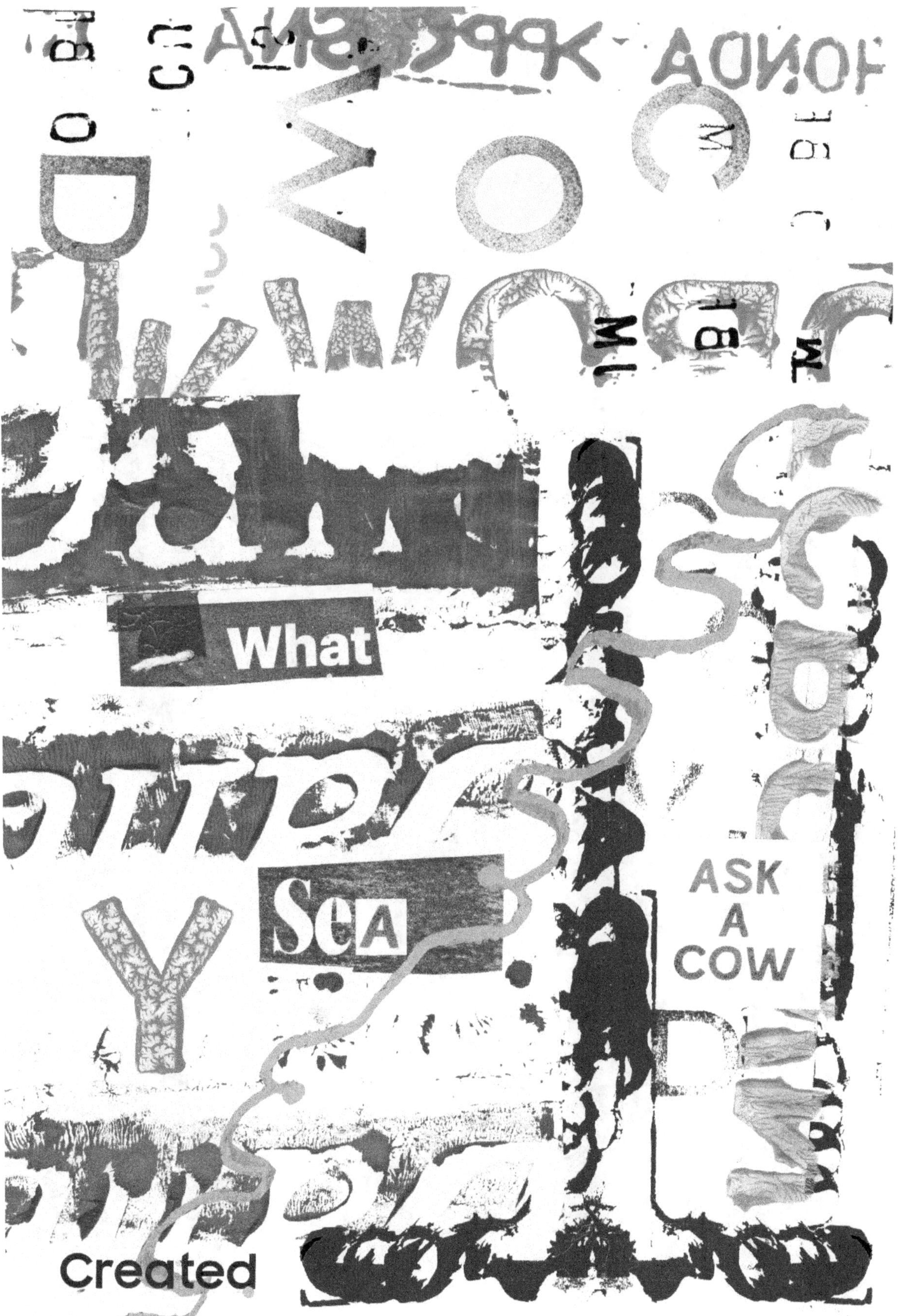
What
SeA
ASK
A
COW
Created

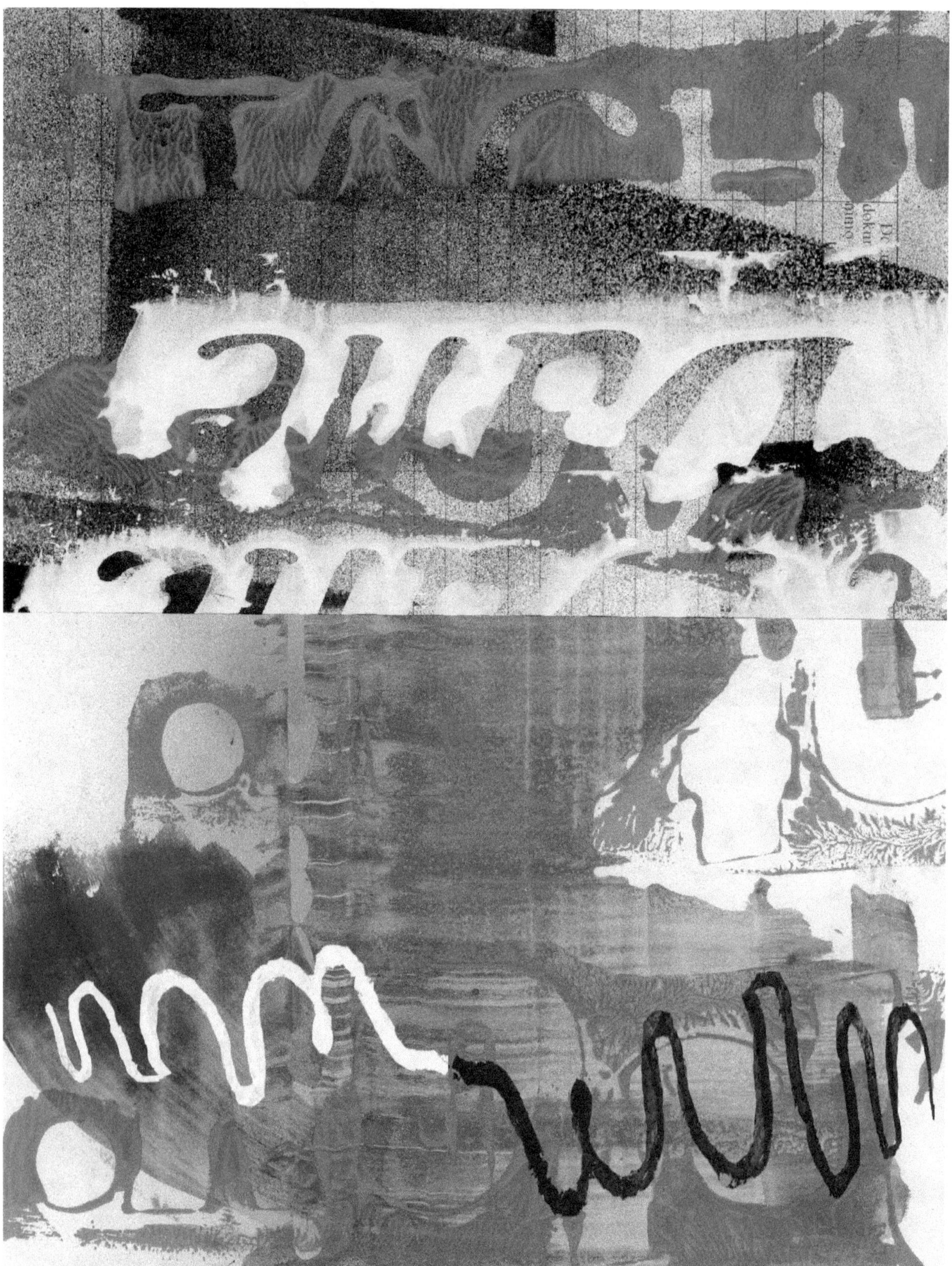

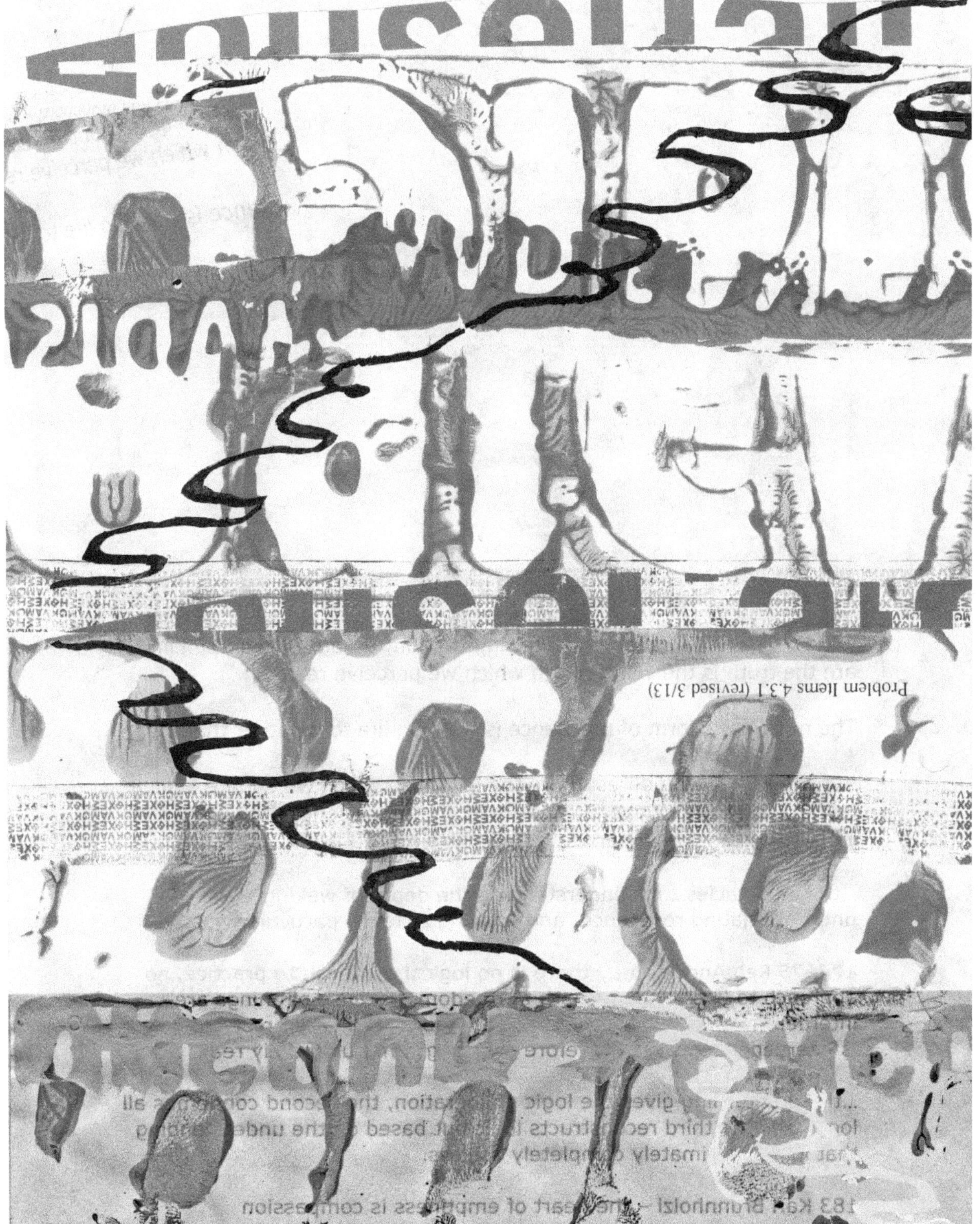

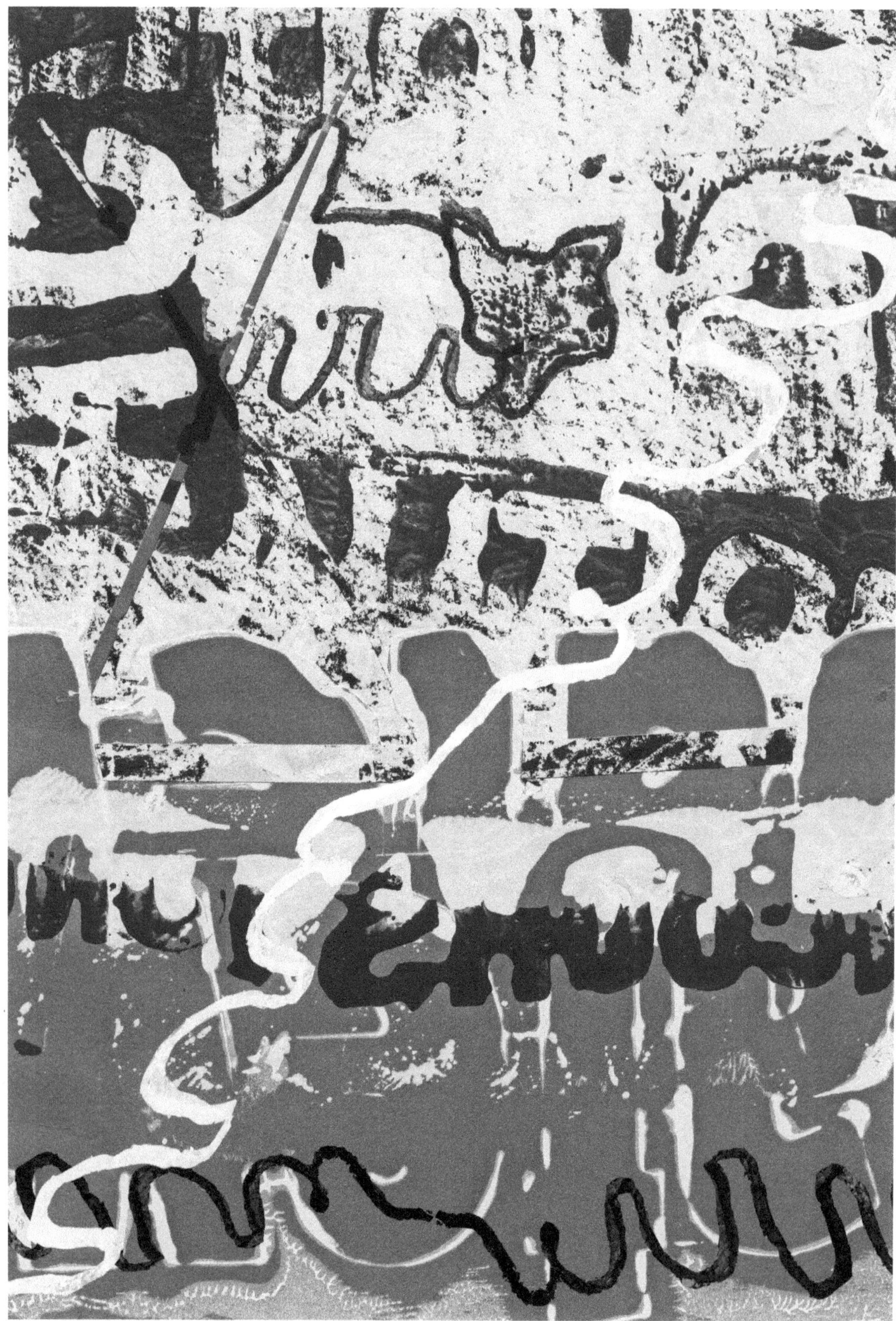

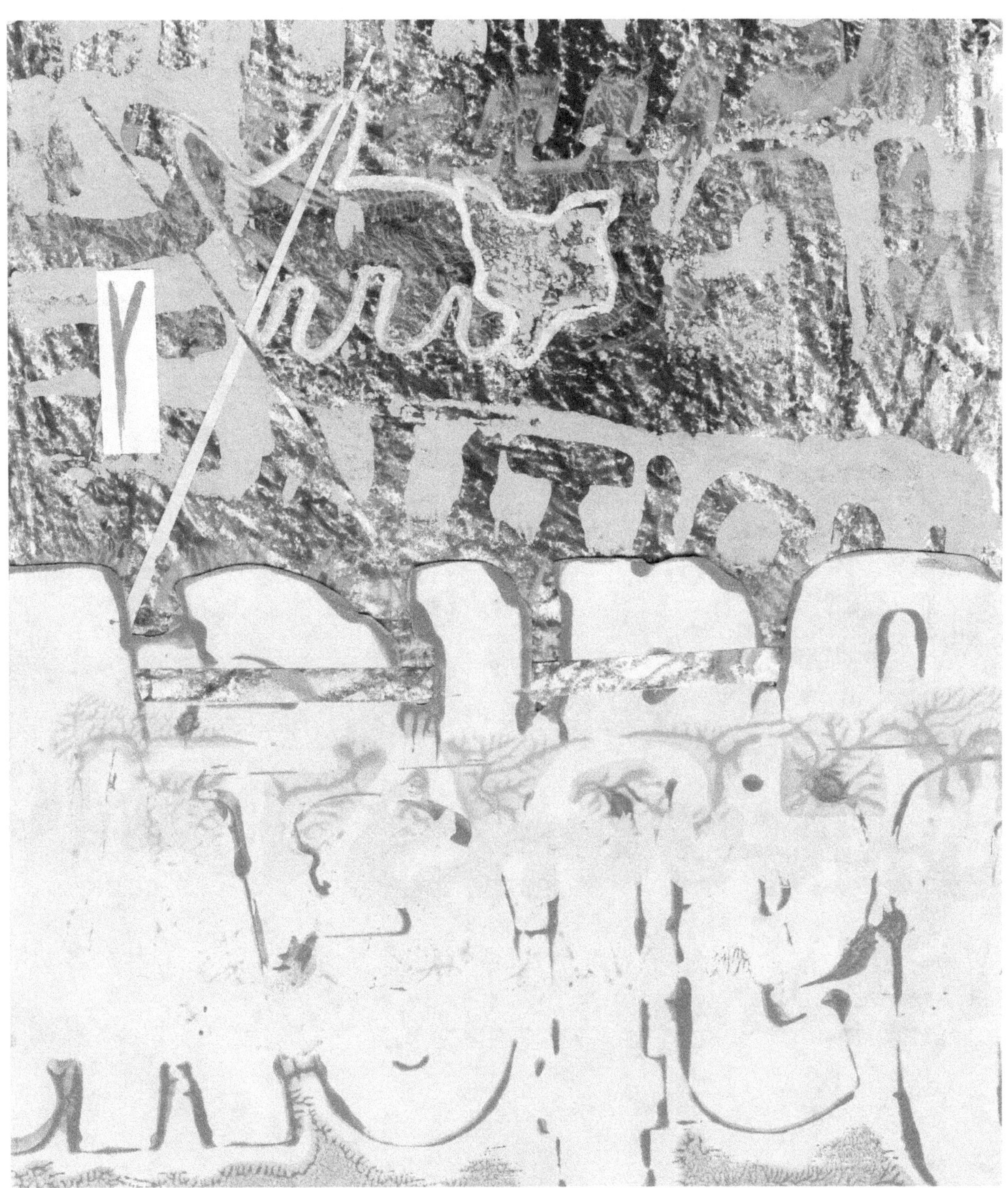

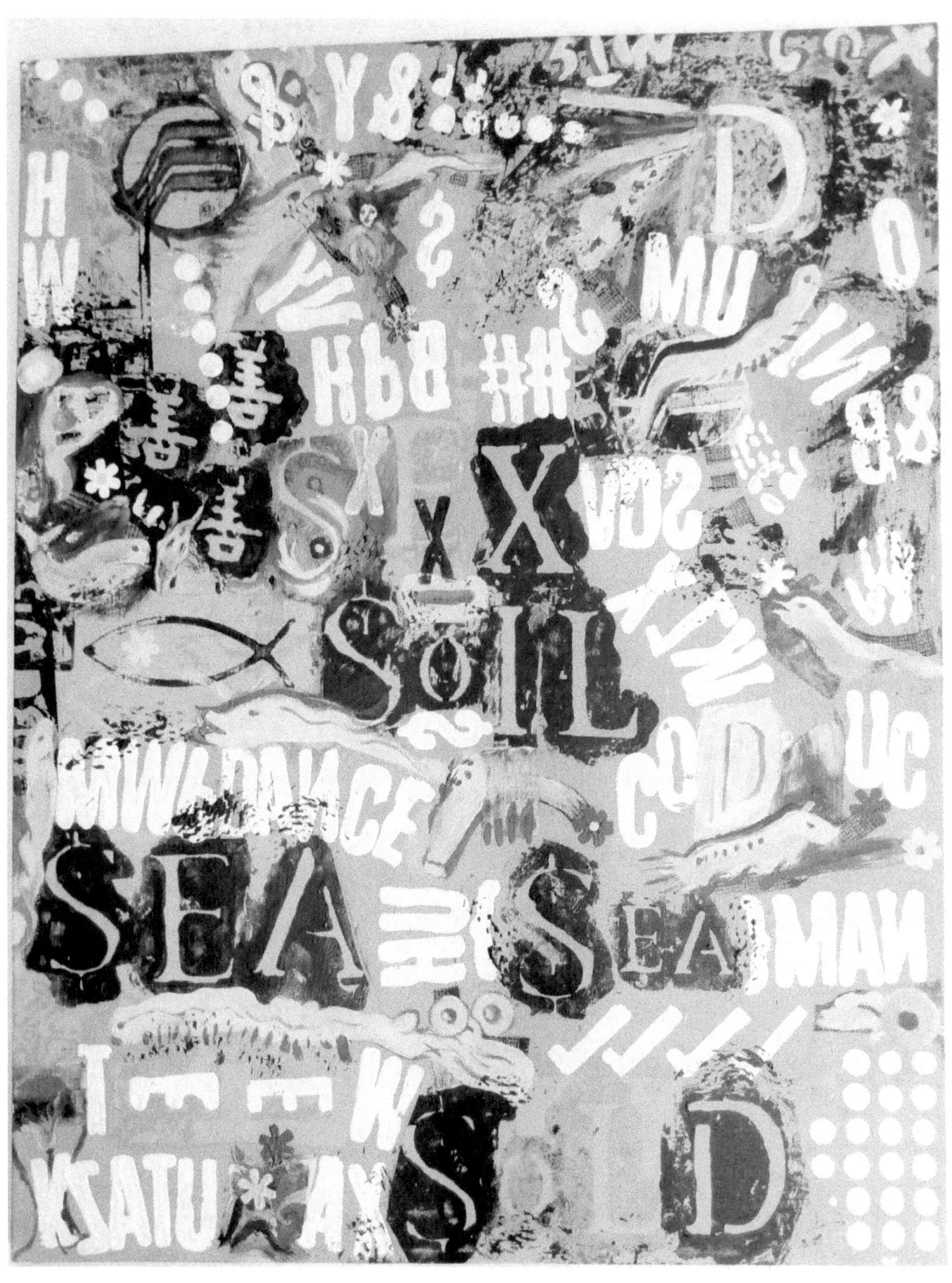

Soilent Sea

Collaborations with John M. Bennett

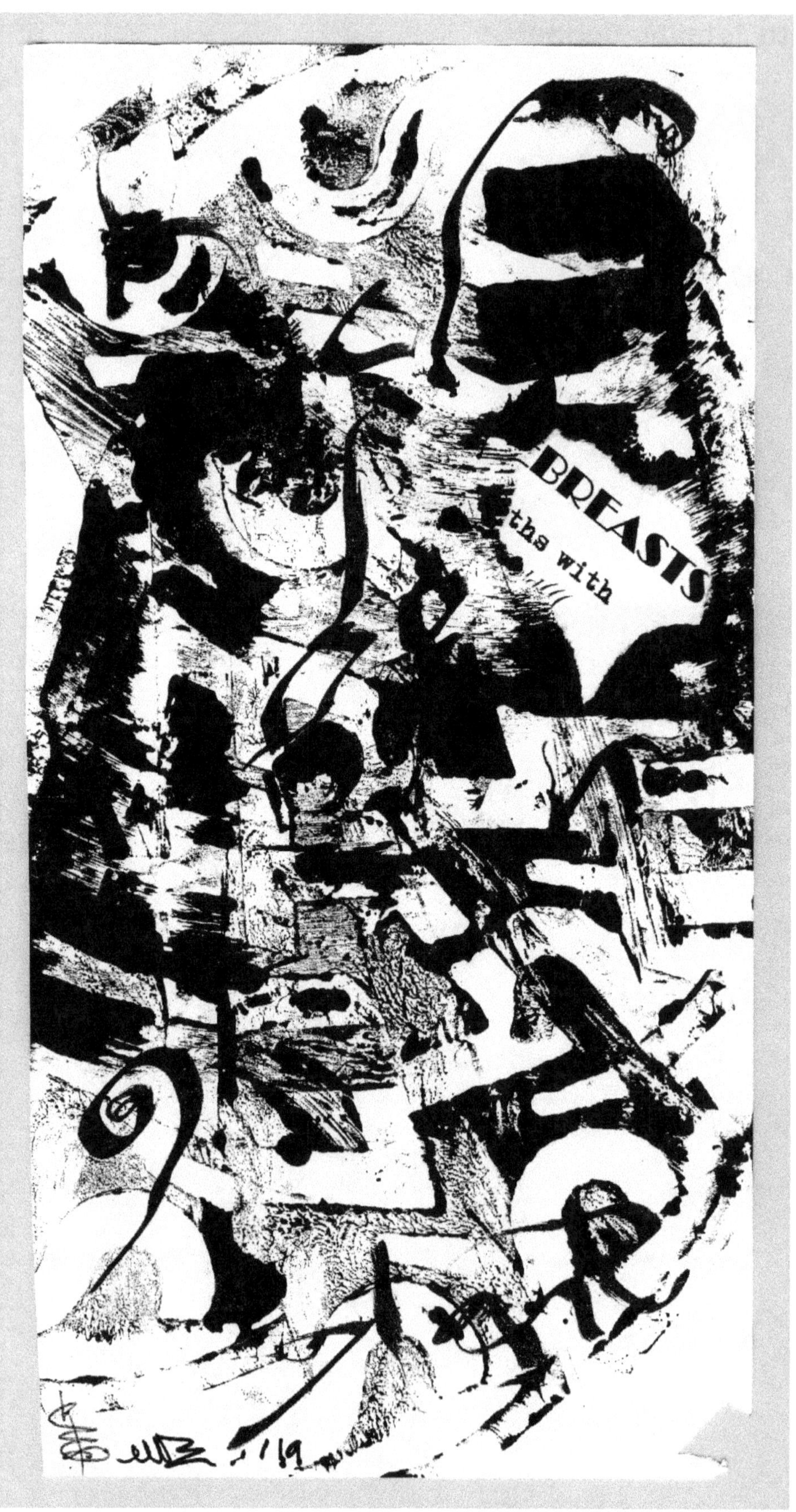
BREASTS
ths with

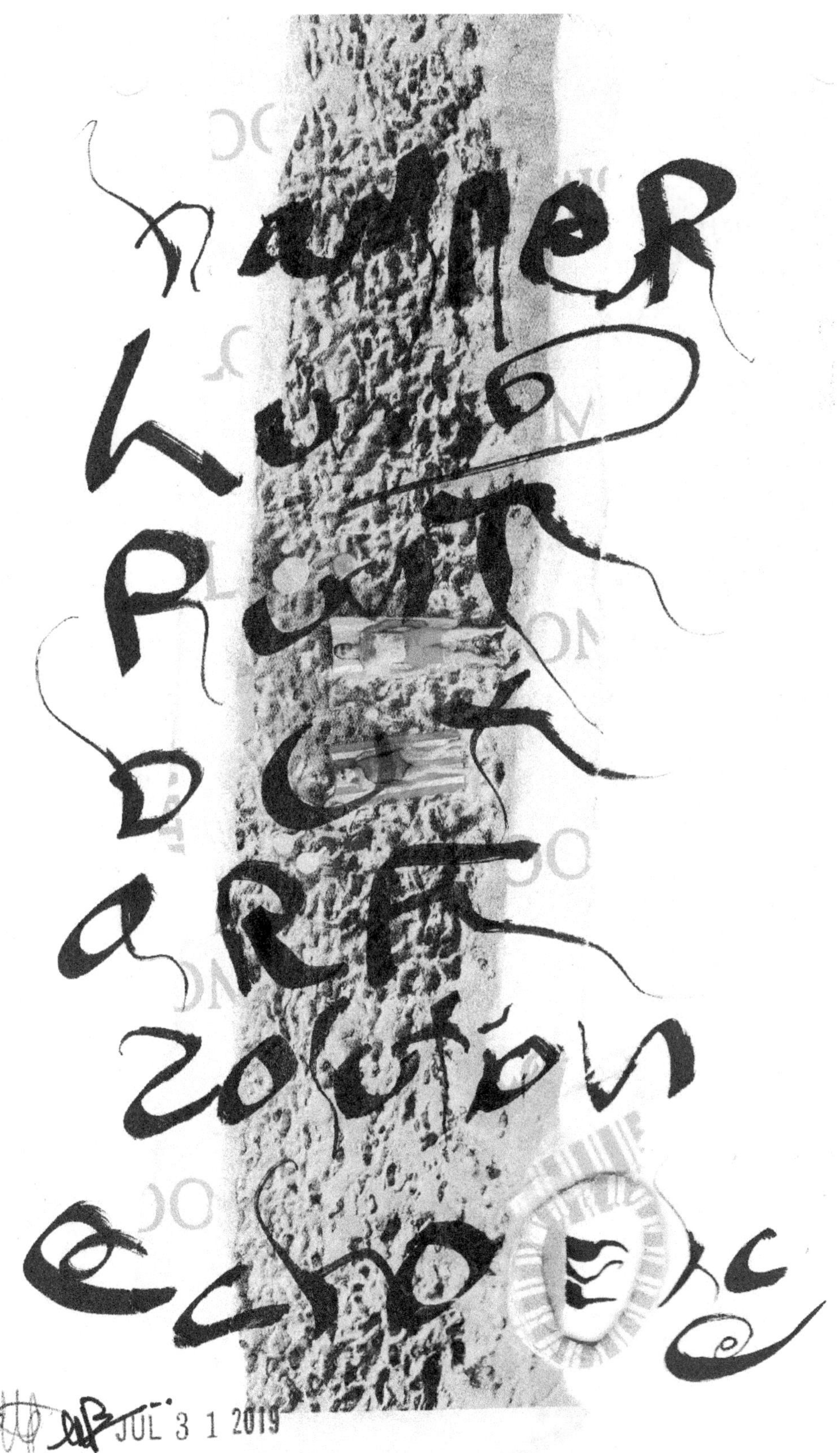
JUL 3 1 2019

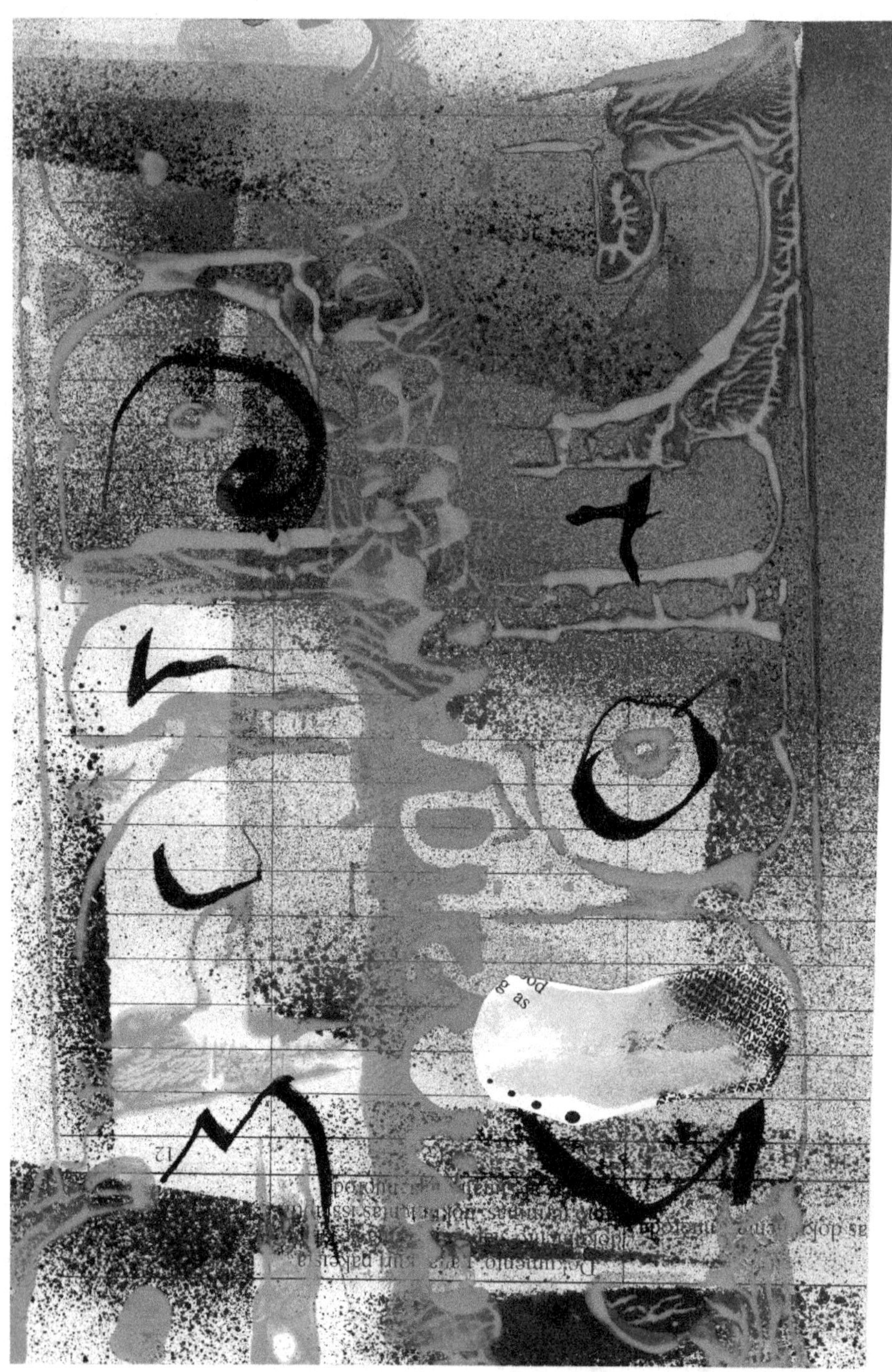

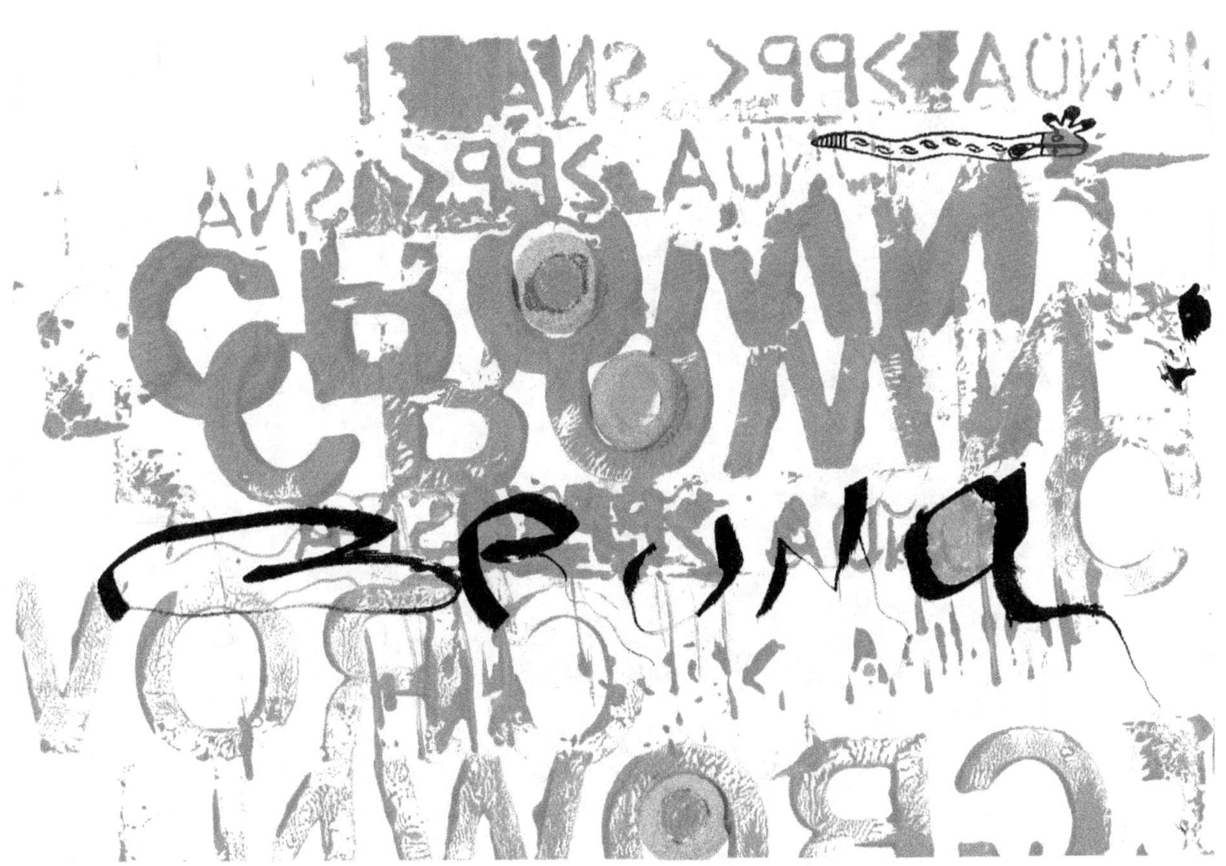

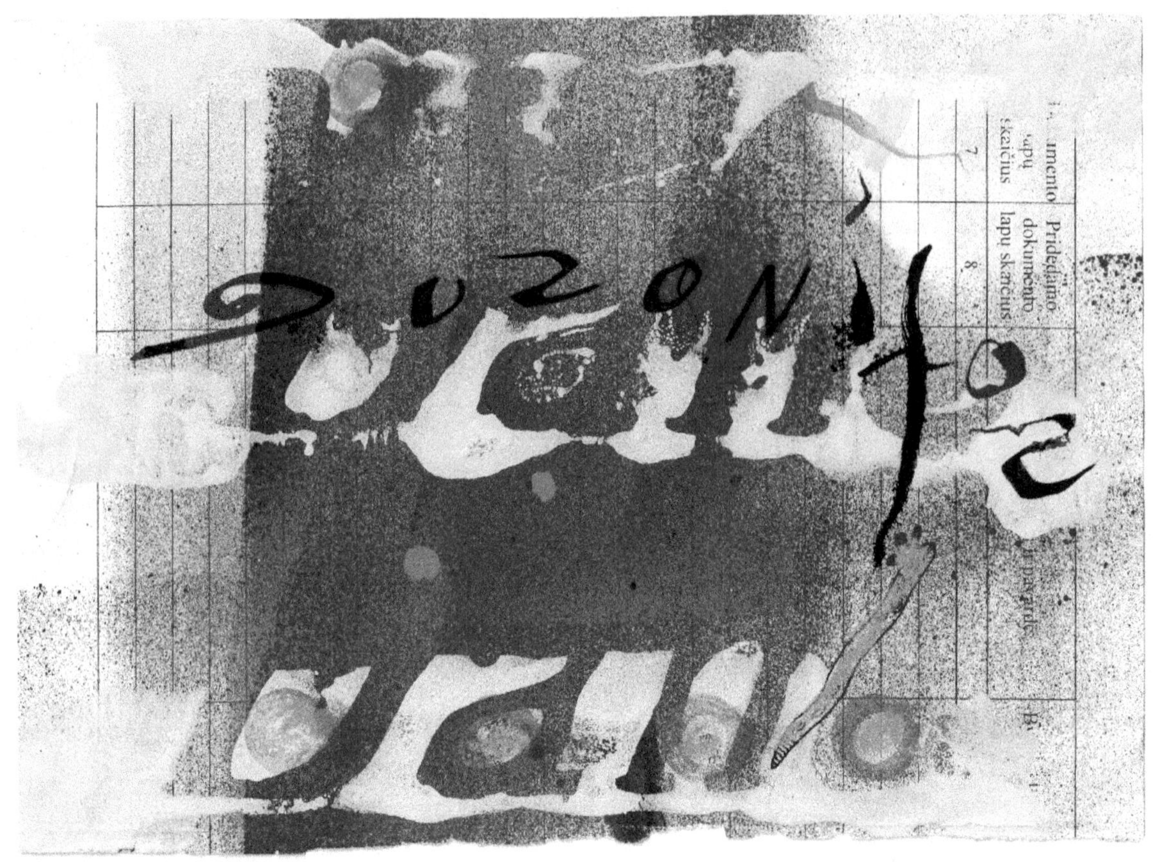

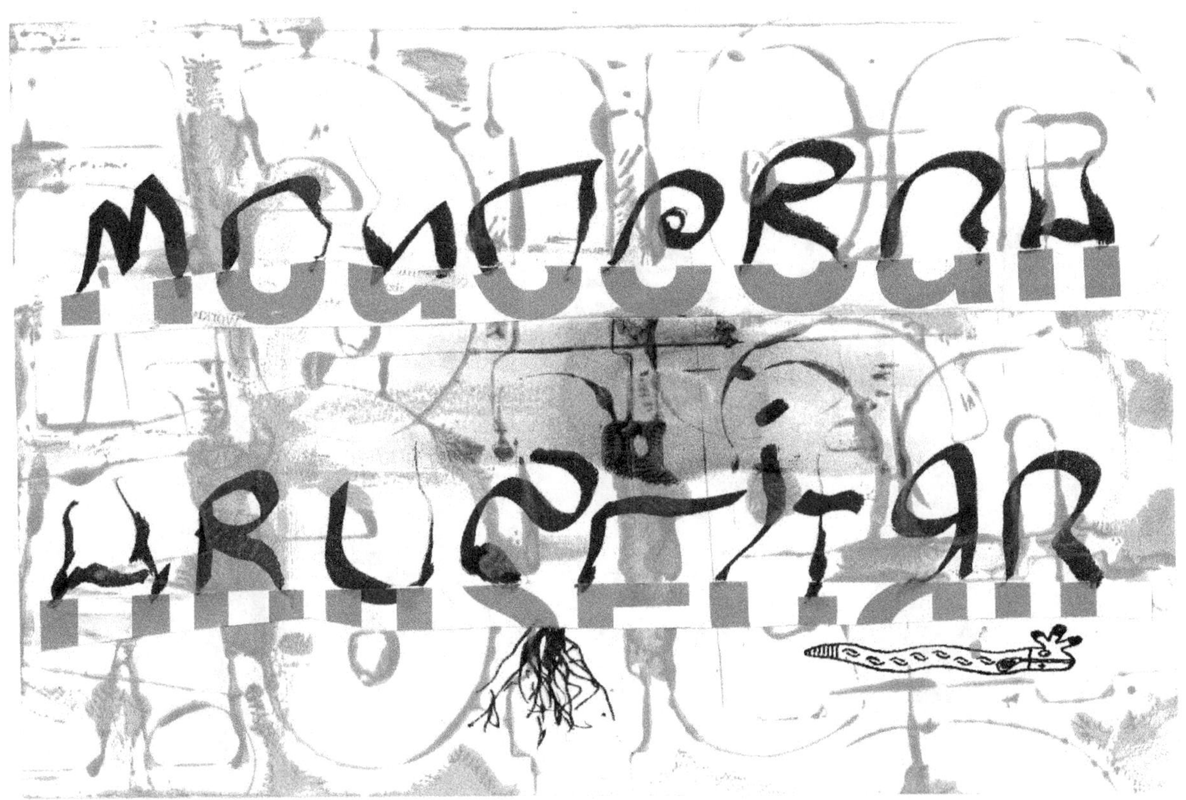

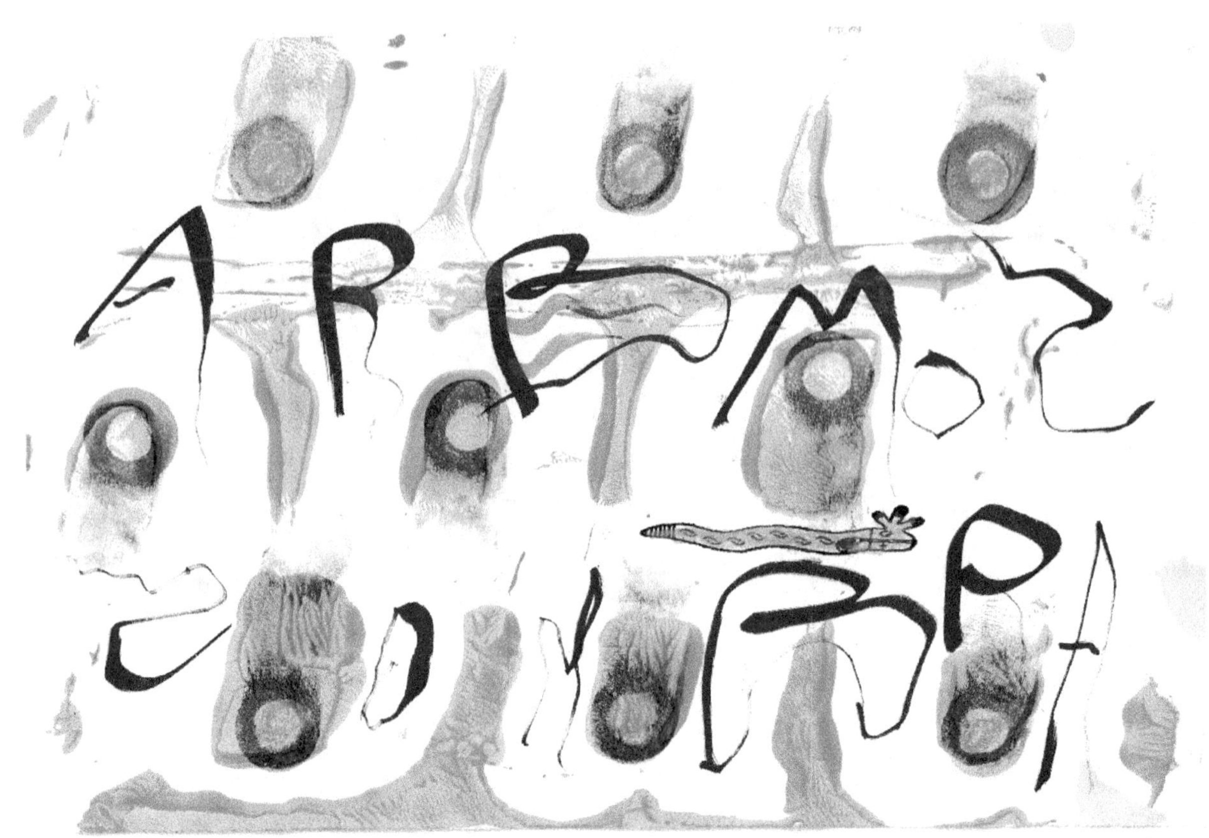

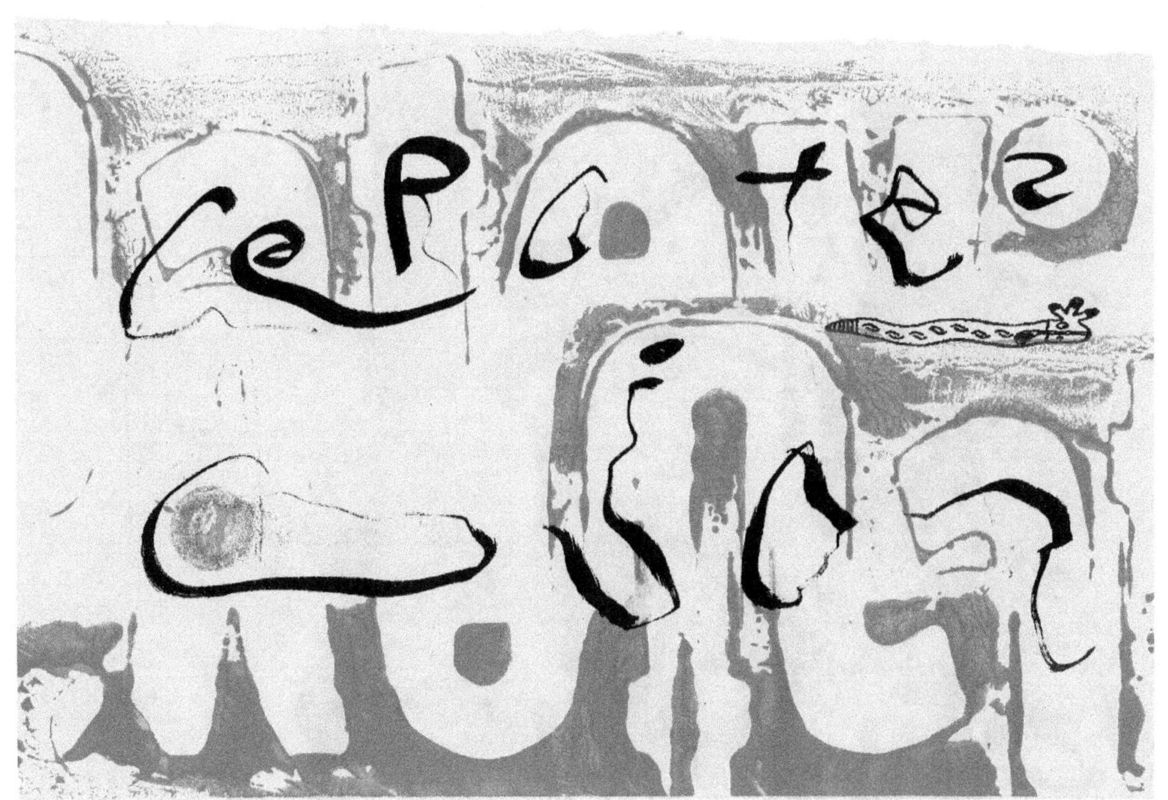

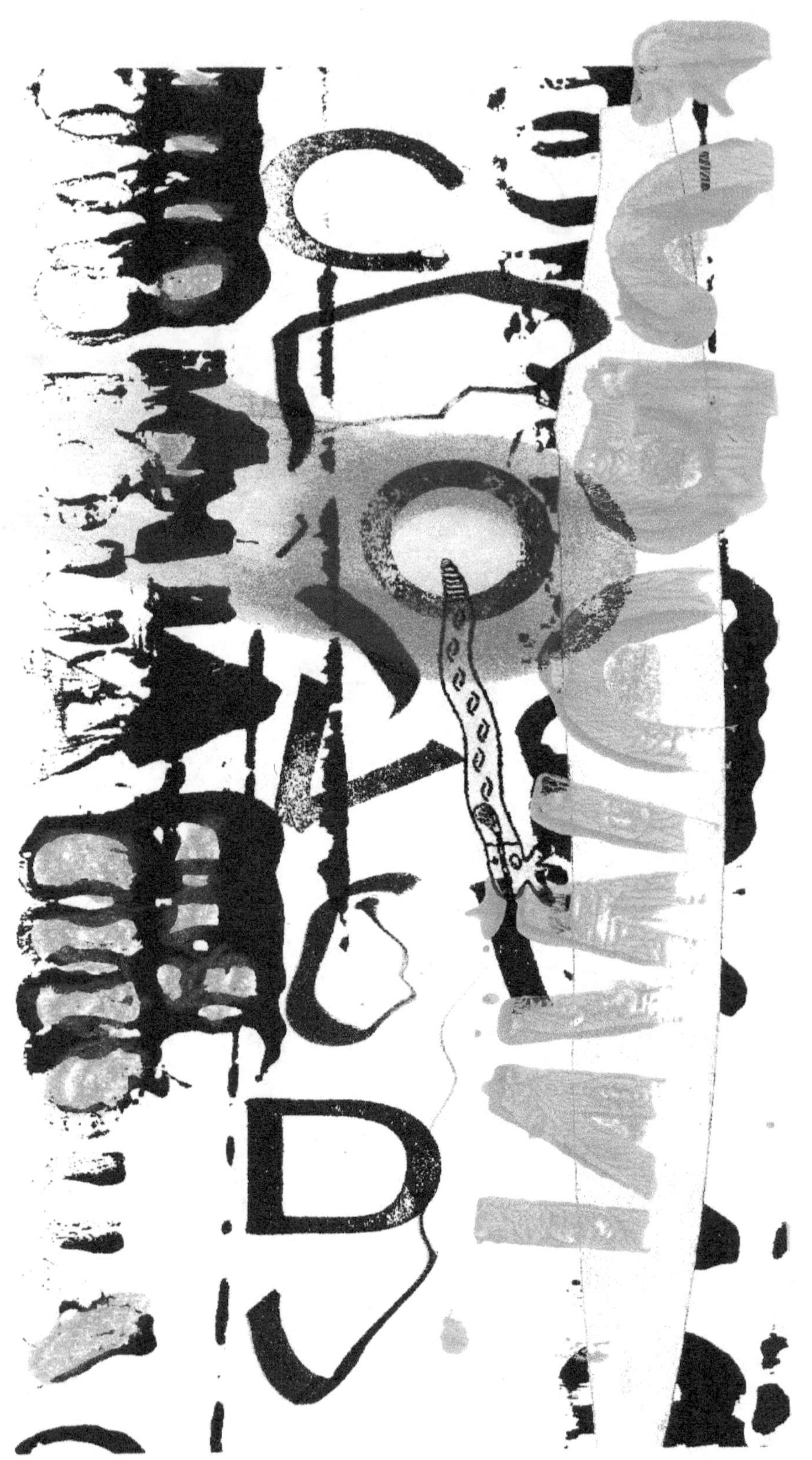

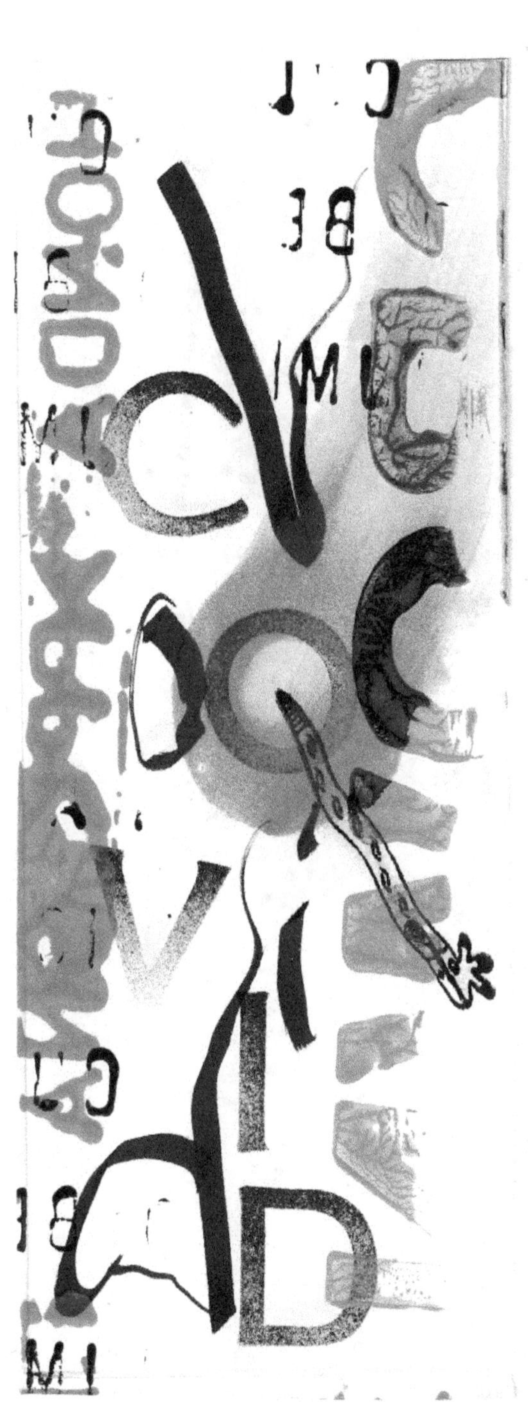

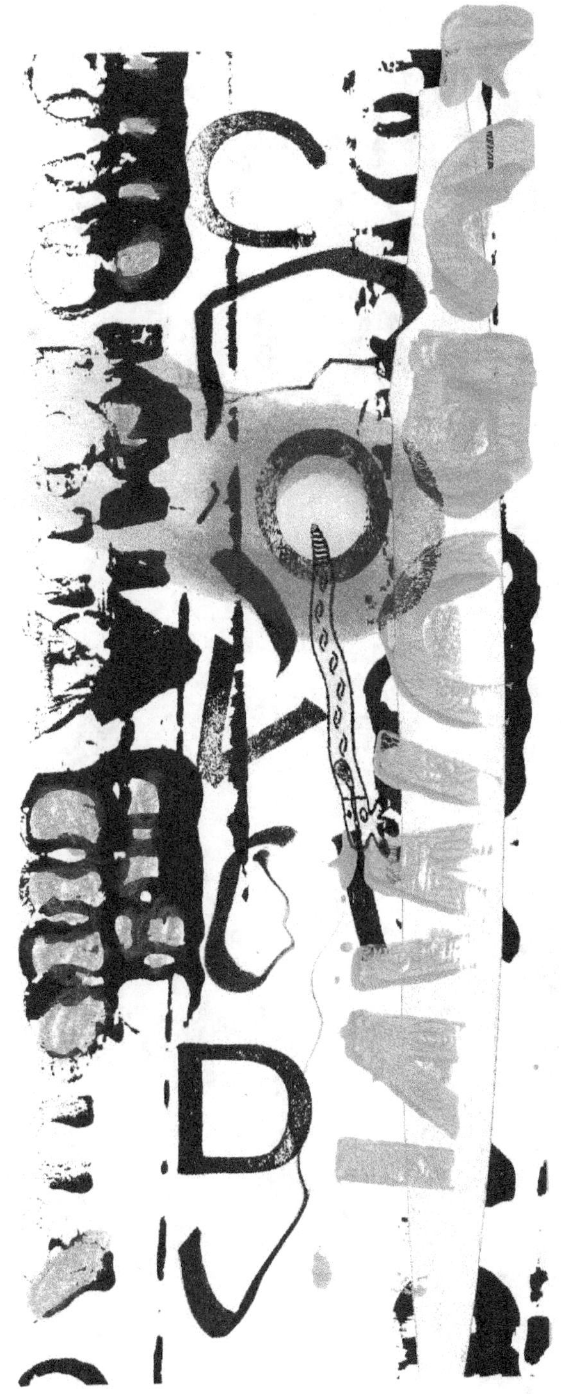

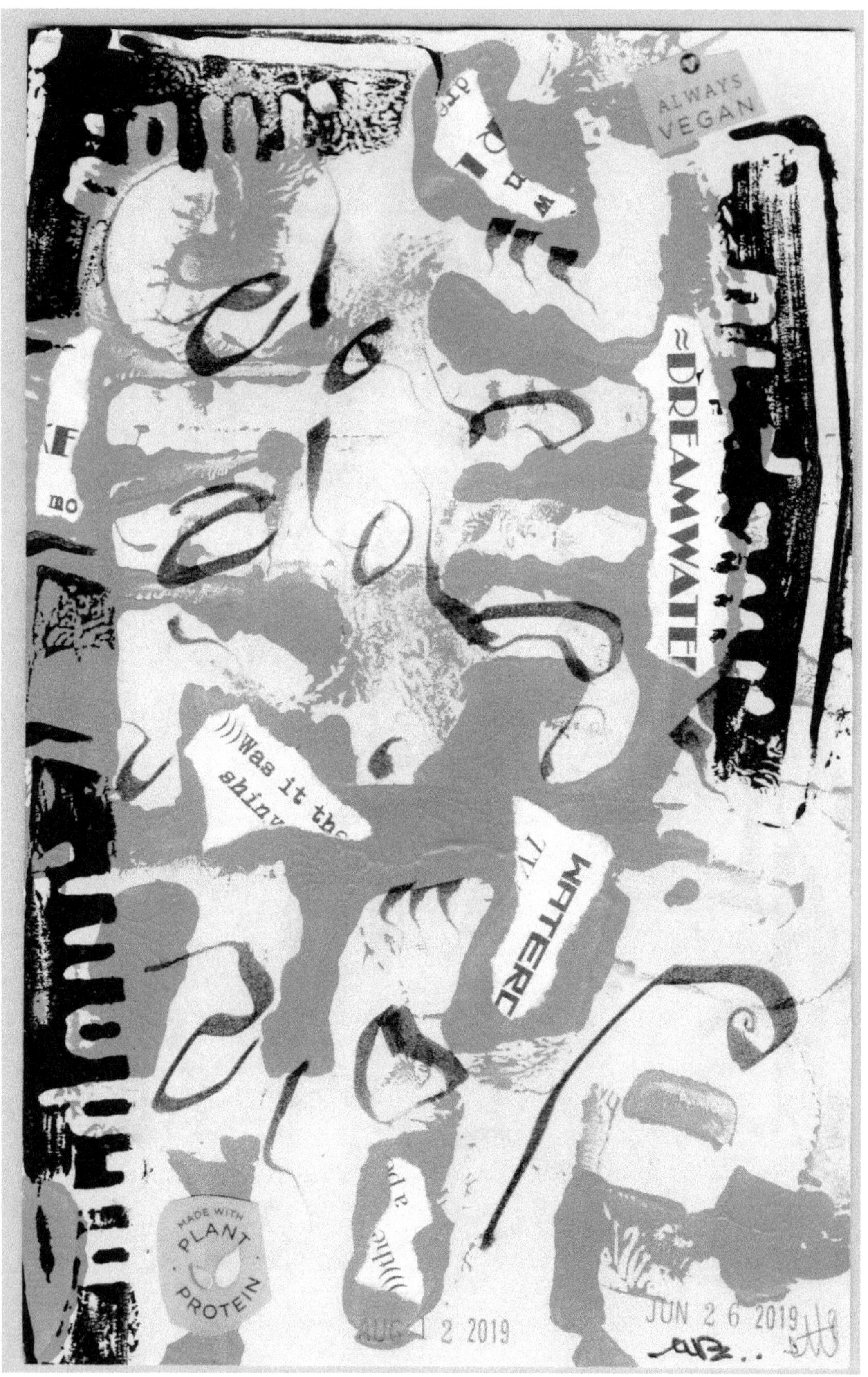
ALWAYS VEGAN
DREAMWATER
Was it the shiny
WATERC
MADE WITH PLANT PROTEIN
AUG 1 2 2019
JUN 2 6 2019

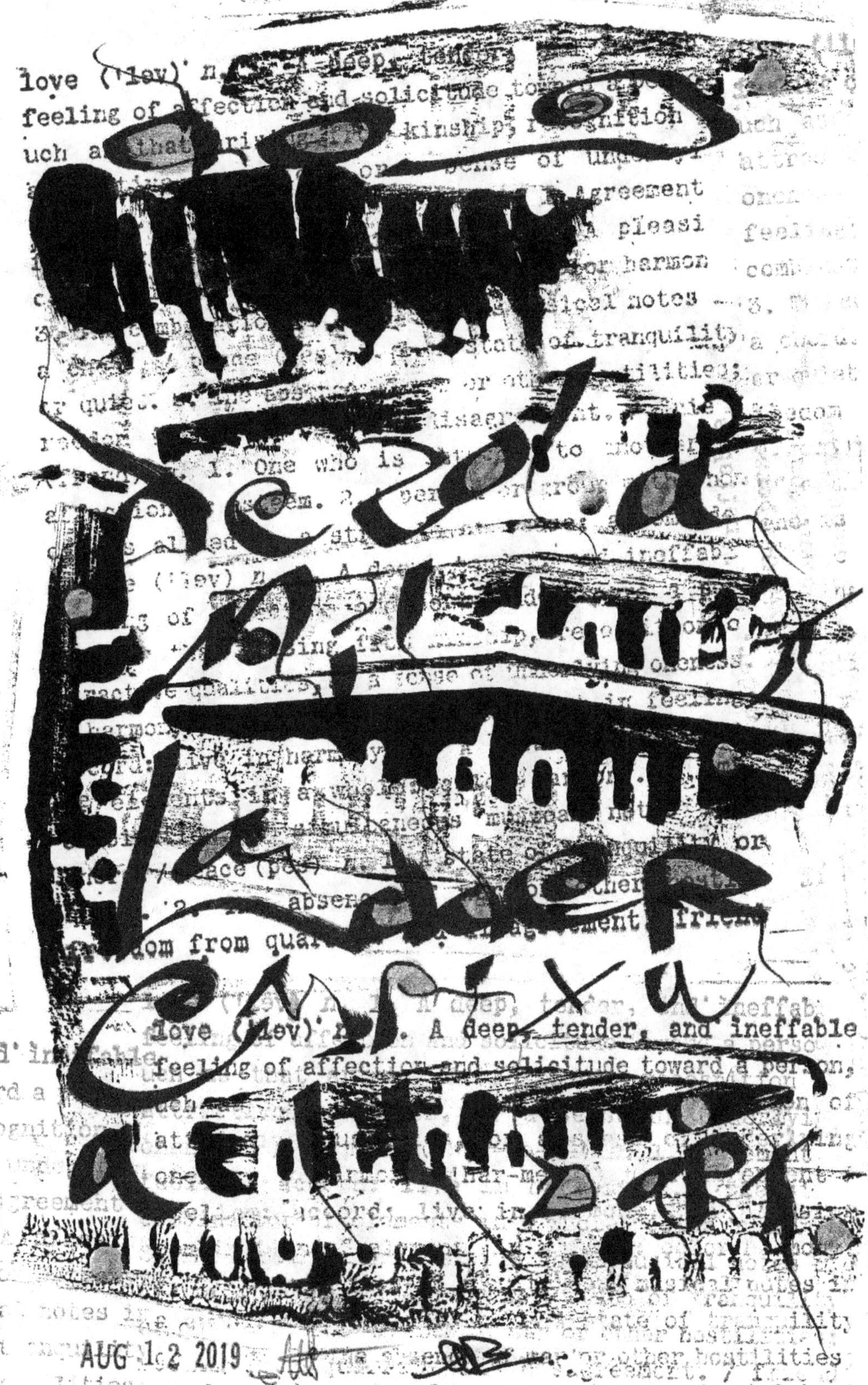

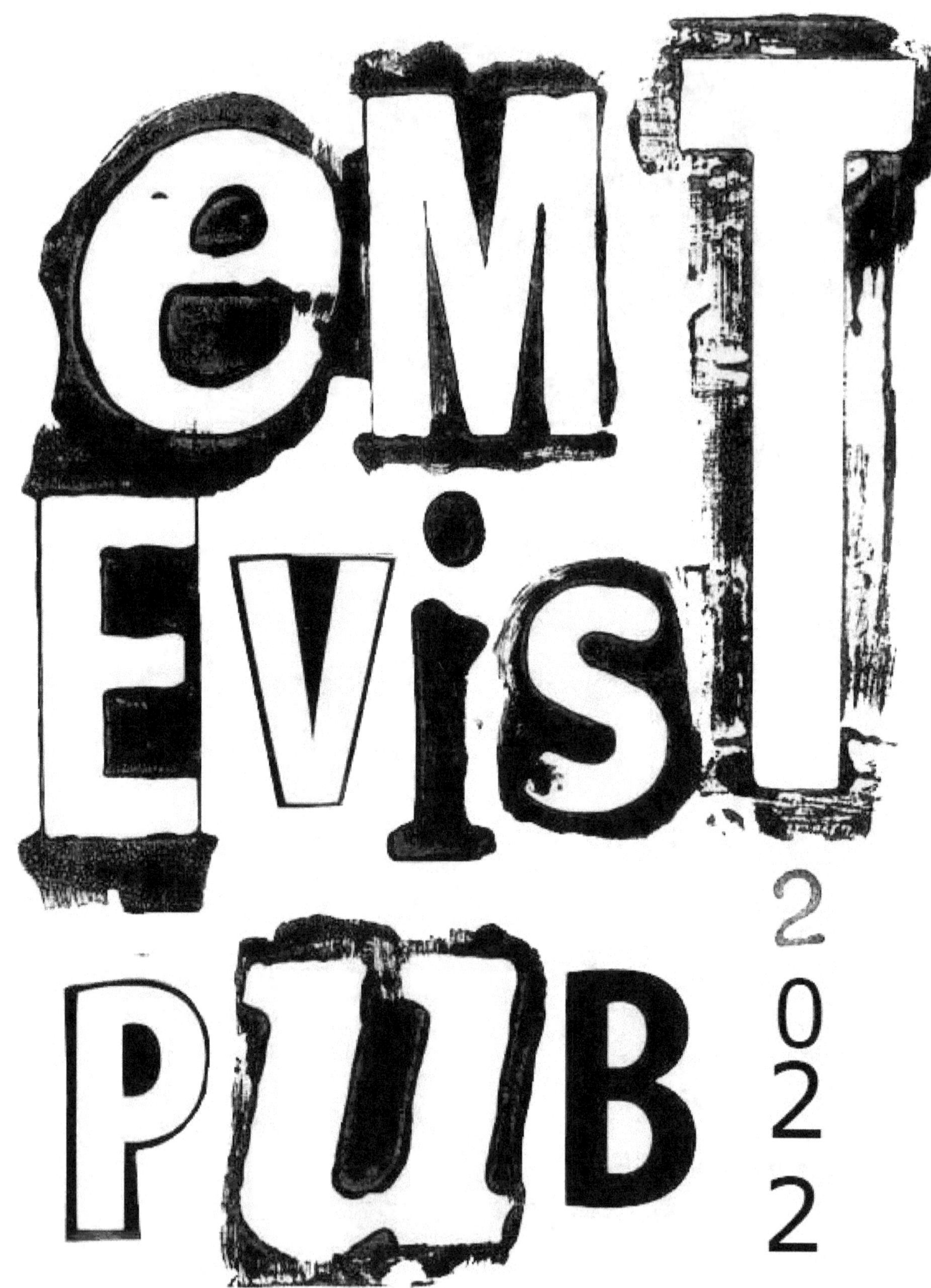
eMT
EViS
PUB
2022

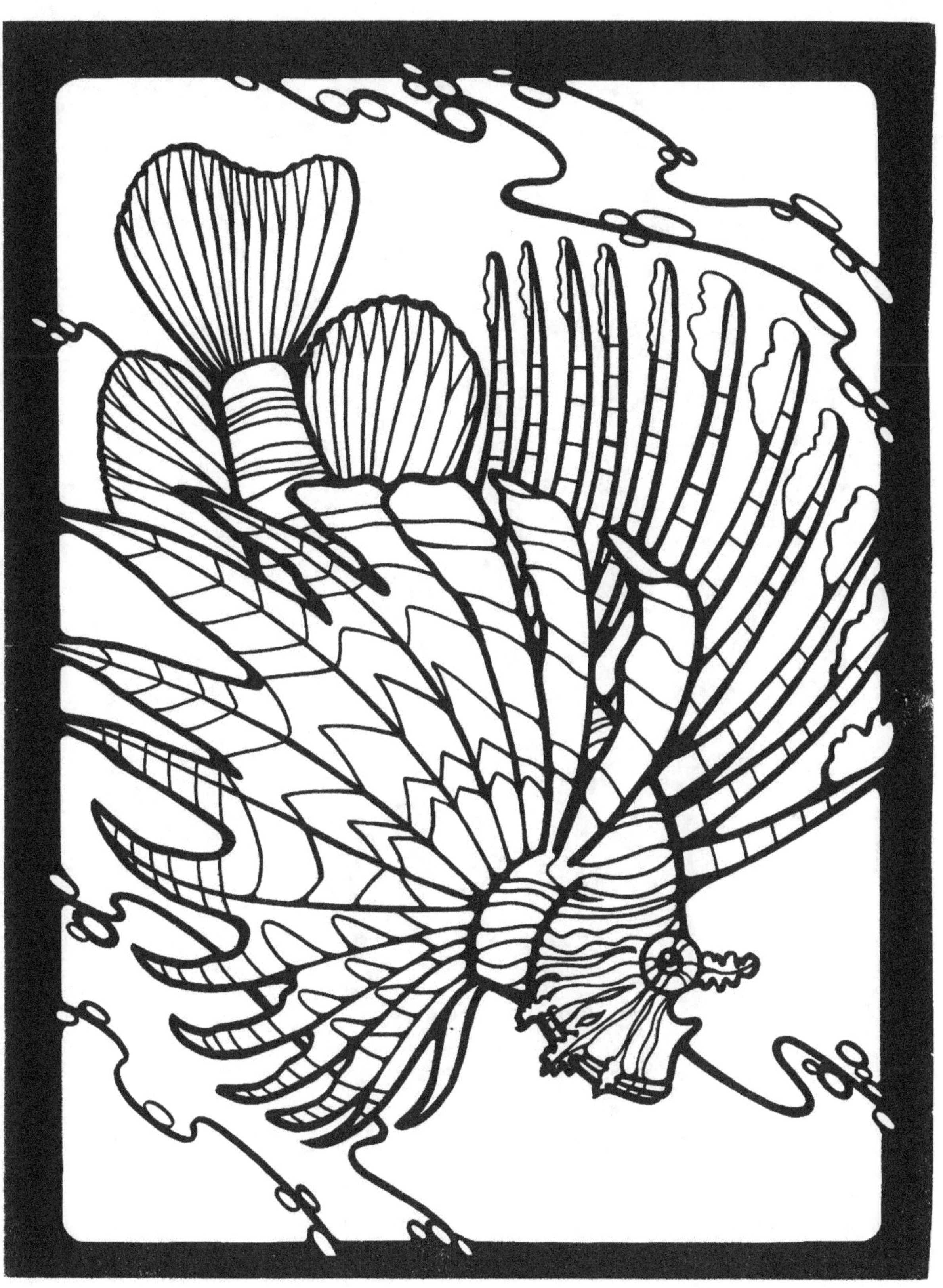

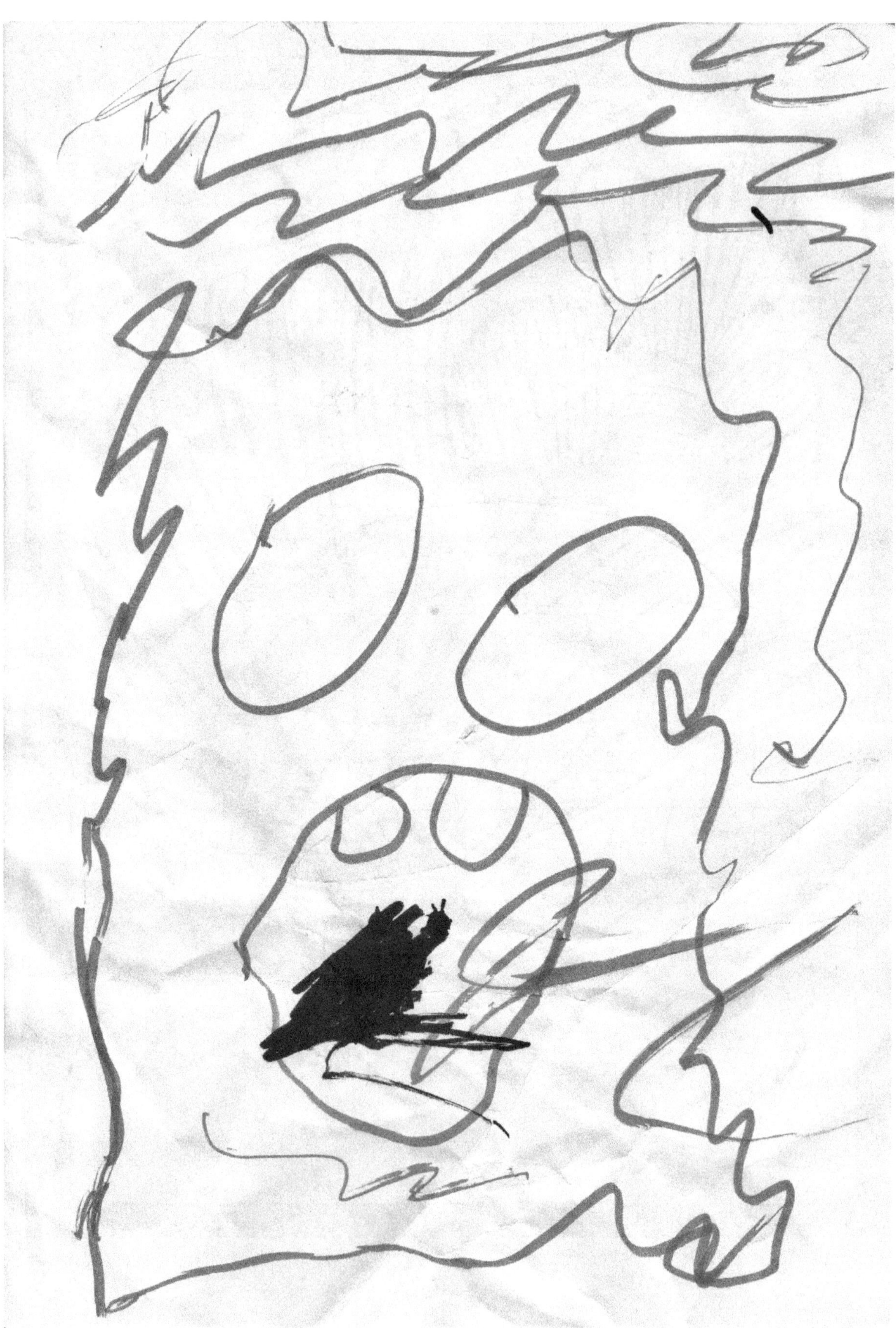

www.ingramcontent.com/pod-product-compliance
Lightning Source LLC
LaVergne TN
LVHW061251100826
845148LV00008B/1099
* 9 7 8 1 7 3 5 3 8 5 0 4 4 *